SIMPLY *Special*

RECIPES FOR FAMILY AND FRIENDS

PATRICK ANTHONY

SIMPLY
Special

RECIPES FOR
FAMILY AND FRIENDS

Hodder & Stoughton
LONDON SYDNEY AUCKLAND TORONTO

British Library Cataloguing in Publication Data

A catalogue record for this book is
available from the British Library

ISBN 0-340-42535-0

Photographs by Simon Smith

Published by Hodder and Stoughton,
a division of Hodder and Stoughton Ltd,
Mill Road, Dunton Green, Sevenoaks, Kent TN13 2YA
Editorial Office: 47 Bedford Square, London WC1B 3DP

Photoset by SX Composing, Rayleigh, Essex

Printed in Great Britain by Butler & Tanner Ltd, Frome and London

*This book is dedicated with affectionate thanks
to Delia Smith, who encouraged me to do it.*

Jane Judd my understanding literary agent.

*Christine Medcalf my Editor who has the
patience of a Saint.*

*And especially to my wife Vanessa, for
everything.*

CONTENTS

INTRODUCTION

This collection of recipes will, I believe, provide regular inspiration and help for anyone who needs or wants to cook, whether it be for family, friends, special occasions, weekend treats or personal interest. Additionally there are no difficult techniques involved or impossible ingredients to acquire.

Overall there is today a wider choice of good quality fresh food available than ever before and this book will enable you to take full advantage of this.

Of course, too, there are huge numbers of pre-prepared and cooked 'meals' on the multiple-store shelves, temptingly convenient to re-heat and serve. Putting cost to one side, these products have a worthwhile role to play, especially as so many of us today have been nudged into the fast lane of life. However, I think we should all 'pull-over' now and then, otherwise we shall come to the end of the road having missed much of the best scenery. Cooking, as well as food, can be enjoyed rather than endured and for millions already it has become a weekend hobby, providing a pleasurable distraction from daily responsibilities, with the added bonus of a worthwhile treat and feeling of satisfaction at the end.

My selection here includes, under ten main headings, recipes for all occasions at home, together with a handful of useful sauces and teatime snacks.

There is also a section devoted to vegetarian main courses which are well worth trying whether you're a meat-eater or not. I am certain that this book can become your indispensable kitchen companion and earn you the everlasting gratitude of family and friends. Happy cooking.

THE QUESTION OF VEGETABLES TO ACCOMPANY MAIN DISHES

As far as I am concerned this question can be answered in one word *seasonal*, because this is when they are at their freshest and best tasting, and in most cases steaming is the ideal cooking method to employ, with a last minute dressing of light seasoning and melted butter. The following is a short list of mostly home-grown vegetables, well worth seeking out at the appropriate time of year.

JANUARY
Beetroot, celeriac, leeks, onions, spinach

FEBRUARY
Salsify, shallots, Brussels sprouts

MARCH
Carrots, spring greens, spring onions, root vegetables, calabrese

APRIL
Spring cabbage, carrots and new season Jersey Royal potatoes (an expensive treat)

MAY
Asparagus, early broad beans, primo cabbage, spinach

JUNE
Asparagus, new potatoes, green beans, early globe artichokes, courgettes

JULY
Fresh peas* (although sadly the best may have gone to be deep frozen), green beans, broad beans

AUGUST
Courgettes, tomatoes, peppers, sweetcorn (of which I consider only the frozen, imported variety to truly live up to its name, since I've never come across a fresh home bought example that tastes as good)

SEPTEMBER
Early wild mushrooms, cauliflower, carrots

October
Autumn cabbages, broccoli, marrows, early turnips and a wide variety of squashes which deserve wider popularity than they enjoy at present

November
Parsnips, red and savoy cabbages, celery, leeks, carrots, cauliflower, turnips

December
Curly kale, swedes, spinach, Brussels sprouts, leeks

*The nicest peas are usually taken by the frozen pea companies, however I have found that to get the best possible flavour and texture from frozen peas you should ignore the packet cooking instructions and simply place them directly into a lidded saucepan with 1 tablespoon of water and 1 oz (25 g) of butter per half pound of peas, and allow them to gently defrost and heat through completely, then serve immediately. This doesn't take many minutes so time everything else accordingly.

'WHICH OIL SHOULD I USE?'

Over the past fifteen years I have been regularly asked which is the best oil for cooking and my response has always been to recommend groundnut (peanut) oil, since it will tolerate much higher temperatures than any other oil, which is particularly important when preparing stir-fry dishes Also when a mixture of oil and butter is called for, this is particularly helpful, since butter alone will burn and turn black unless great care is taken.

Most retailers and supermarkets now stock a good range of oils, including a wide range of olive oils, which may vary in nationality and style, so it is difficult to recommend particular types as some can be very strong and fruity and even peppery. If you happen to buy one you don't really care for, blending it with sunflower oil can help to make it more palatable.

Label Information:

Extra Virgin Olive Oil
This is the best quality oil obtained by simple cold pressing of the natural fruit.

Olive Oil and Pure Olive Oil
Some olive oils after pressing may contain excessive acidity, flavour or colour and need to be refined and blended with virgin olive oil before being suitable for consumption.

Other Oils
It's worth noting I think, that virgin olive oil alone is the only totally naturally produced oil – (5 kilos of olives to make 1 litre) and all other vegetable and seed oils have to be 'treated' before they are fit to eat.

Apart from the long familiar corn, sunflower and 'vegetable' oils, walnut and hazelnut oils in particular can add a great deal of interest to salads, either straight or mixed with one of the others, according to taste and experimentation.

Sesame Oil
Distinctive dark brown oil, made from roasted sesame seeds which is often called for in Chinese stir-fry recipes. A little goes a long way and a few drops only can be added to salad dressings for a change.

FIRST COURSES

Avocado Soup

½ medium onion
1 clove garlic, crushed
1 large, ripe avocado
juice of ½ lemon
1 pint (570 ml) tomato juice
salt and pepper
2" (5 cm) piece of cucumber,
    with skin, finely diced
chopped parsley to garnish

YOU COULD CALL THIS DELIGHTFUL SOUP MEXICO'S ANSWER TO SPAIN'S GAZPACHO. IT'S IDEAL FOR SUMMER EATING AND I LIKE TO ADD A DASH OF TABASCO SAUCE FOR EXTRA INTEREST.

Grate the peeled onion finely on to a plate, to catch the juice. Mix the crushed garlic in with this.

Peel the avocado and mash the flesh in a large bowl. Beat in the onion with garlic, and the lemon juice. Pour in the tomato juice and mix well. Season to taste.

Chill in the fridge and just before serving stir in 6 ice cubes.

Garnish each portion with a little cucumber dice and some chopped parsley.

~

French Onion Soup

SERVES 6

6 very large onions
3 oz (75 g) butter
salt and pepper
½ teaspoon brown sugar
1 level tablespoon flour
3 pints (1.75 litres) beef stock
2 tablespoons brandy (optional)
Parmesan cheese, grated

I FIRST TASTED THIS AGED ABOUT FOURTEEN AND I'VE NEVER FORGOTTEN THE PLEASURE IT GAVE ME AND THE WARM HAPPY GLOW OF SATISFACTION IT PRODUCED.

Peel the onions, and slice them thinly in rings. Heat the butter in a saucepan until it begins to foam. Then add the onions, cover the pan and cook over a gentle heat for 10 minutes. Add seasoning and the sugar. Sprinkle with flour and cook for a further 3 minutes, stirring all the time. Slowly stir in the stock (and brandy, if using) and when well mixed cover the pan and continue cooking gently for about 30 minutes.

Serve each portion topped with a generous handful of grated Parmesan cheese.

~

SERVES 4

1 oz (25 g) butter
1 tablespoon oil
4 oz (110 g) streaky bacon,
  finely chopped
1 medium onion, finely chopped
2 sticks celery, finely chopped
2 cloves garlic, crushed
2 tomatoes, skinned and
  chopped
6 oz (175 g) carrots, diced
salt and pepper
2½ pints (1.5 litres) beef stock
1 teaspoon dried marjoram or
  oregano
8 oz (225 g) leeks, finely sliced
6 oz (175 g) cabbage, shredded
1 dessertspoon tomato purée
15 oz (425 g) can red kidney
  beans, drained
2 tablespoons broken spaghetti
2 tablespoons parsley, chopped
2-3 oz (50-75 g) Parmesan
  cheese, fresh if at all possible,
  and much better if you can
  buy a piece and fine grate it
  yourself

Minestrone

ASK ANYONE TO NAME AN ITALIAN SOUP AND THEY ARE SURE TO ANSWER MINESTRONE! IN FACT THAT COUNTRY OF TRULY GREAT FOOD HAS DOZENS OF SOUPS TO ITS CREDIT AND EQUALLY THERE ARE AS MANY RECIPES FOR MINESTRONE AS THERE ARE PASTA SHAPES. THIS IS MY FAVOURITE.

In a large saucepan, heat the oil and butter and gently cook the bacon, onion, celery and garlic for a minute or two. Then add the tomatoes and carrots with some salt and pepper. Cook gently for about 10 minutes, stirring occasionally.

Next pour in the stock and dried herbs, followed by the leeks and cabbage. Simmer, covered, for 1 hour, then add tomato purée, beans and broken spaghetti.

Cook for a further 30 minutes. Remove from the heat and stir in the chopped parsley.

Serve with the grated Parmesan cheese on the side.

~

Fish Chowder

SERVES 4

1 lb (450 g) fresh haddock
salt and pepper
1 tablespoon wine vinegar
2 rashers lean bacon, de-rinded
    and chopped
1 onion, sliced
14 oz (396 g) can tomatoes
2 potatoes, peeled and diced
½ pint (275 ml) fish or chicken
    stock
bay leaf
2 whole cloves
¼ pint (150 ml) milk
chopped parsley to garnish

FOR ME, THIS BIG-HEARTED AMERICAN-STYLE SOUP IS A MEAL IN ITSELF AND THE PERHAPS SURPRISING NOTION OF COMBINING BACON WITH FISH HAS VERY SUCCESSFULLY STOOD THE TEST OF TIME AND TASTE. JUST BE CAREFUL WITH THE SEASONING, ACCORDING TO PREFERENCE.

Poach the haddock gently in water seasoned with salt and pepper and wine vinegar, for about 10 minutes. Remove the fish from the pan, reserving the cooking liquid if wished, and flake the cooked fish, discarding any skin or bones.

In a pan, fry the bacon until the fat begins to run. Add the onion and cook for about 5 minutes, but do not allow the onion to brown. Add the flaked fish, with the tomatoes and cubed potatoes. Pour over the ½ pint (275 ml) of stock, using reserved liquid if wished, and add the bay leaf, whole cloves and salt and pepper to taste.

Simmer gently for 30 minutes then add the milk, removing the bay leaf and the cloves. Reheat very gently and serve piping hot sprinkled with chopped parsley.

~

Seafood and Sweetcorn Chowder

SERVES 6

8 oz (225 g) cod fillet
2 oz (50 g) butter
1 large onion, chopped
¼ teaspoon fennel seeds
12 oz (350 g) can sweetcorn
1½ pints (850 ml) chicken or
    vegetable stock
salt and pepper
1½ pints (850 ml) milk
4 oz (110 g) cockles or clams
4 oz (110 g) shelled, cooked
    prawns
chopped parsley and cream
    (optional) to garnish

THE NAME CHOWDER, WHICH WE THINK OF AS AMERICAN, COMES FROM THE FRENCH WORD FOR POT (CHAUDIÈRE) AND TRADITIONALLY REFERS TO A THICK, HEAVY SOUP. THE MOST FAMOUS KIND IS CLAM CHOWDER, WHICH USUALLY INCLUDES SALT PORK AS A FLAVOURING. MY VERSION MAY NOT BE STRICTLY AUTHENTIC BUT IT HAS THE SAME SIMPLE, SOOTHING EFFECT.

Skin the cod fillet and cut the flesh into small cubes.

Melt the butter in a large pan and gently cook the onion until soft. Add fennel seeds, sweetcorn, stock and salt and pepper to taste. Simmer gently for 15 minutes. Blend the mixture in a blender or food processor until 'coarsely' smooth. Return to the saucepan and add the milk and cod cubes, and bring to the boil. Return at once to simmering point and add the shellfish. Continue to simmer for just 2 minutes.

Serve at once, garnishing with chopped parsley and a dash of cream, if liked.

Quick Pea Soup

UNLESS YOU GROW YOUR OWN YOU'LL BE VERY LUCKY INDEED TO FIND YOUNG, TENDERSWEET PEAS AVAILABLE, SO TOP QUALITY FROZEN ARE YOUR BEST BET AND YOU'RE WELCOME, AS I DO, TO DOUBLE THE QUANTITY OF CRUNCHY CROÛTONS AS THEY'RE IRRESISTIBLE.

SERVES 4

1½ lb (700 g) green peas, shelled or frozen
1 medium onion, very finely chopped
1 lettuce, sliced
2 oz (50 g) butter
salt and pepper
½ teaspoon sugar
1½ pints (850 ml) light stock
1 egg yolk
3 tablespoons single cream
2 thick slices white bread, cubed

Put the peas, onion and lettuce in a pan with the butter. Cover the pan and cook very slowly indeed until the vegetables are tender – about 20-25 minutes. Rub through a sieve or liquidise, then return to the pan. Add the seasoning, sugar and stock. Simmer for 10 minutes.

In a small bowl mix the egg yolk with the cream and blend with a little of the hot soup. Return the mixture to the pan and heat gently, but do not allow to boil.

Fry the bread cubes in a little hot butter until golden and crisp.

Serve the soup, floating the croûtons on the top at the last moment.

~

Asparagus Flamande

THIS BUTTER, EGG, LEMON AND CHIVE DRESSING ADDS WELCOME IN-TEREST TO FRESHLY STEAMED ASPARAGUS – ESPECIALLY THE LESS FLAVOURSOME IMPORTED VARIETY.

SERVES 4

2 lb (900 g) asparagus
2 hard-boiled eggs
2 tablespoons fresh chives, chopped
2 dessertspoons parsley, finely chopped
6 oz (175 g) butter
2 tablespoons lemon juice
salt and pepper

Steam the asparagus over a pan of boiling water until cooked but still with a little firmness.

Shell the hard-boiled eggs and either chop them very finely or grate them.

In a bowl toss together the eggs, chives and parsley.

In a small pan melt the butter then remove from the heat and allow to cool slightly. Pour into a warmed serving dish, leaving behind as much of the white sediment as possible.

Add the lemon juice and salt and pepper to taste to the melted butter and stir in one-third of the egg and herb mixture.

Arrange the warm asparagus on a serving dish and sprinkle over the remaining two-thirds of the egg and herb mixture. Serve immediately accompanied by the delicious butter sauce.

Asparagus Tarts

for the pastry
6 oz (175 g) plain flour
pinch of salt
1½ oz (40 g) lard
1½ oz (40 g) margarine
cold water to mix

for the filling
4 oz (110 g) shallots or onion
2 oz (50 g) butter
1 clove garlic, crushed
20 young asparagus tips
2 egg yolks
4 fl oz (110 ml) double cream
salt and pepper
grated nutmeg

THE THINNER, CHEAPER ASPARAGUS SPEARS ARE IDEAL HERE AND IN WINTER YOU CAN SUBSTITUTE SLENDER SLICED LEEKS. THE SEASONED 'CUSTARD' FILLING IS ABSOLUTELY DELICIOUS ESPECIALLY WHEN THE TARTS ARE SERVED WARM.

Preheat the oven to 350°F-180°C-Gas Mark 4. For the pastry, sift the flour and salt into a bowl. Rub in the fats until the mixture resembles breadcrumbs, and mix in a little water to make a smooth dough. Chill for 20 minutes before using. Grease 4 × 3" (7.5 cm) individual tart tins and line with greaseproof paper, add baking beans and bake 'blind' for 10 minutes. After the 10 minutes remove the paper and beans and return the cases to the oven for a further 5 minutes.

Increase the oven temperature to 375°F-190°C-Gas Mark 5. For the filling chop the shallots or onion very finely. Melt the butter and soften the shallots with the garlic. Remove from the heat and when cool spread a quarter of the mixture in the base of each tart case.

Trim the asparagus tips so each one is about 1½" (4 cm) long. Steam the asparagus for a few minutes only, then run under the cold tap, to refresh them. Pat dry on kitchen paper.

Place 5 asparagus tips in each tart case, pointing out from the centre like the spokes of a wheel. Beat together the egg yolks and double cream. Season with salt, pepper and nutmeg and pour a quarter of this over each tart filling.

Place the tartlets on a baking tray and cook in the oven for about 20-25 minutes until just set and light brown on the top.

~

Cabilla Cream

1 medium smoked mackerel (or
    4 fillets)
2 hard-boiled eggs
1 teaspoon made horseradish
    sauce
1 tablespoon finely chopped
    chives
5 fl oz (150 ml) soured cream
freshly ground black pepper
pinch cayenne pepper

I'M NOT QUITE CERTAIN WHERE THIS RECIPE ORIGINATED, BUT I CAN SAY THAT ON FIRST ACQUAINTANCE A FEW YEARS AGO, I WAS IMMEDIATELY IMPRESSED AND TIME HAS NOT DIMINISHED ITS APPEAL. THIS ALSO MAKES A VERY ENJOYABLE CANAPÉ TOPPING.

Remove the skin from the smoked mackerel, and if necessary, slide the fillets off the bone. Flake the flesh gently with a fork.

Peel and chop the hard-boiled eggs.

Fold the mackerel, eggs, horseradish sauce and chives into the soured cream. Add freshly ground black pepper before spooning the mixture into four small ramekin dishes. Sprinkle the top with a pinch of cayenne pepper.

Serve with hot salted biscuits. (I use Ritz Crackers.)

~

Country Pâté

5-6 rashers streaky bacon
½ oz (10 g) flour
½ oz (10 g) butter
¼ pint (150 ml) milk
4 oz (110 g) belly pork
4 oz (110 g) pig's liver
1 oz (25 g) onion
4 oz (110 g) pork sausagemeat
1 clove garlic, crushed
2 tablespoons dry sherry or
    brandy
salt and pepper
1 bay leaf

A SPLENDID SUPPLY OF HOT TOAST AND A GLASS OR TWO OF ORDINARY RED WINE ARE ALL THAT'S NEEDED TO COMPLETE THIS COSY KITCHEN TABLE FEAST.

Remove the rind from the bacon and flatten each rasher with the blade of a knife, then use to line a 1 pint (570 ml) loaf tin.

Place the flour, butter and milk in a saucepan. Heat together, whisking continuously, until the sauce thickens.

Mince the pork, liver, onion and sausagemeat together twice and add to the sauce. Stir in the garlic and sherry and season to taste with salt and pepper. Turn the mixture into the lined loaf tin and top with the bay leaf. Cover with a lid or foil and stand in a roasting tin half filled with water. Cook in the oven at 350°F-180°C-Gas Mark 4 for 1 hour.

Let the pâté become cold in the tin before turning out. Then leave for a day in a cold place for the flavours to develop. Serve sliced with hot toast – delicious.

~

Eggs Mimosa

I'VE NEVER KNOWN ANYONE TO REFUSE THIS ATTRACTIVE-LOOKING LITTLE DISH AND THE HANDY HINT FOR MAYONNAISE-THINNING AT THE END OF THE RECIPE (ESPECIALLY FOR THE BOUGHT-IN-JARS KIND) IS WELL WORTH KNOWING.

SERVES 4

6 hard-boiled eggs
1 red pepper
4 oz (110 g) prawns, shelled
juice of ½ lemon
6 tablespoons mayonnaise
salad leaves
4 black olives

Shell the hard-boiled eggs and cut in half, removing the yolks carefully and keeping on one side. De-seed the red pepper and chop finely.

In a bowl mix together the prawns, red pepper, lemon juice and 2 tablespoons of the mayonnaise. Stuff the egg whites with this mixture and place carefully, flat side down, on to a serving plate.

Spoon the remainder of the mayonnaise over the top of the eggs. Arrange some salad leaves around the side of the dish.

Place the reserved egg yolks in a sieve and holding the sieve over the serving plate push the yolks gently through the sieve to cover the top of the mayonnaise. Slice the olives thinly and place at intervals along the top of the eggs.

Note: If your mayonnaise seems a little thick to pour over the top of the eggs, mix in 2 tablespoons of boiling water and stir well and it will produce a smooth coating consistency.

~

Mushrooms à la Grecque

SERVES 4

1 lb (450 g) button mushrooms
1 onion, peeled
8 oz (225 g) tomatoes
4 tablespoons olive oil
¼ pint (150 ml) dry white wine
bouquet garni
1 clove garlic, peeled
salt and freshly ground black
    pepper
chopped parsley

I REMEMBER 'MAKE ROOM FOR THE MUSHROOMS' AS A CLEVER SLO-
GAN PROMOTING THE STANDARD COMMERCIAL VARIETY OF MUSH-
ROOM AND THERE'S NO DOUBT THAT THIS CLASSIC TREATMENT
GREATLY INCREASES THEIR INTEREST. USEFUL TOO AS THE WHOLE
THING CAN BE PREPARED WELL IN ADVANCE.

First wipe the mushrooms and remove all the stalks. Chop the
onion finely. Cover the tomatoes with boiling water for about 30
seconds. Remove them and peel off their skins under running
water. Cut them in half and de-seed them.

Heat 2 tablespoons of the olive oil in a pan and sauté the onion
until soft but not coloured. Add the wine, bouquet garni and the
garlic, and season with salt and pepper. Gently stir in the mushrooms and the tomatoes, and continue to cook, uncovered, over a
gentle heat for about 10 minutes. Remove from the heat and allow
to cool.

Remove the bouquet garni and the garlic clove and stir in 2
more tablespoons of olive oil.

Serve chilled, sprinkled with chopped parsley.

~

Prawn Pâté

SERVES 4

6 oz (175 g) peeled, cooked
    prawns, chopped
4 oz (110 g) cream cheese
juice of ½ lemon
1 dessertspoon chopped dill
    weed
salt and pepper
3 spring onions, chopped (white
    part only) or ¼ mild onion,
    chopped

THE ONLY PRAWNS I EVER CONSIDER USING ARE THOSE FROM THE
COLD WATERS OF THE NORTH ATLANTIC OR THE DUBLIN BAY PRAWN
(ACTUALLY NORWAY LOBSTER) SOMETIMES SOLD AS LANGOUSTINE.
THE VARIETY KNOWN GENERALLY AS 'MEDITERRANEAN PRAWNS'
ARE, FOR MY MONEY, OVERSIZED, OVERPRAISED AND OVERPRICED.
THIS SIMPLE PÂTÉ IS SURE TO PLEASE.

Place all the ingredients in the blender or food processor and
blend together until smooth. Serve in individual ramekins with
hot buttered toast.

This makes an ideal topping for canapés too.

~

Prawns with Champagne and Cream

SERVES 2

2 oz (50 g) butter
1 tablespoon spring onion or
   shallot, chopped
3 oz (75 g) small mushrooms,
   sliced
1 glass champagne
1 lb (450 g) peeled, cooked
   prawns
salt and cayenne pepper
1 tablespoon lemon juice
6 fl oz (175 ml) double cream
4 oz (110 g) long-grain rice,
   cooked
chopped parsley and paprika to
   garnish

I'VE GIVEN THIS DISH LITERALLY TO HUNDREDS OF PEOPLE ON LIVE DEMONSTRATION TOURS AND THE RESPONSE IS UNFAILINGLY ENTHUSIASTIC. THE LIST OF INGREDIENTS PLACES IT FIRMLY IN THE 'LUXURY' CLASS BUT FOR A VERY SPECIAL OCCASION YOU COULDN'T DO BETTER, EITHER FOR A FIRST COURSE OR A MAIN DISH. IT'S VERY IMPORTANT NOT TO OVERCOOK THE PRAWNS SO THEY BECOME HARD.

In a pan melt the butter and gently soften the onion. Add the mushrooms and champagne and allow to cook gently for 3 minutes. Add the prawns and heat through. Season with salt and a touch of cayenne pepper. Sprinkle on the lemon juice, followed quickly by the cream.

Blend everything together and when very hot serve over boiled rice, garnished with a dusting of paprika and chopped parsley.

~

Rollmops with Soured Cream Dressing

SERVES 4

4 rollmop herrings
1 onion, very finely diced
1 eating apple, peeled and cored
5 fl oz (150 ml) soured cream
chives, chopped

THIS COULDN'T BE SIMPLER TO PUT TOGETHER AND ALWAYS LOOKS INTERESTING ON THE PLATE. NEEDLESS TO SAY, SOUSED HERRING FANS WILL BE IN HEAVEN.

Allow one rollmop herring per person. (If they are very small, allow two.) Lay the herring flat on the plate, skin side down. Sprinkle a quarter of the raw onion over each fish. Chop the eating apple into small cubes and scatter a quarter of the apple over each fish. Spoon a quarter of the soured cream over the top of each one and cover with fresh chopped chives.

~

SERVES 4

1 lb (450 g) smoked haddock
  fillet
3 fl oz (75 ml) milk
2 hard-boiled eggs
2 oz (50 g) softened butter
½ teaspoon cayenne pepper
½ teaspoon grated nutmeg
½ teaspoon ground mace
salt and freshly ground white
  pepper

Smoked Haddock Mousse

MAKE EVERY POSSIBLE EFFORT TO GET GENUINE SMOKED HADDOCK FOR THIS RECIPE. THIS SHOULD BE A LIGHT BEIGE COLOUR. THE BRIGHT YELLOW FISH JUST ISN'T IN THE SAME CLASS. KEEPING THE MOUSSE IN THE FRIDGE OVERNIGHT IS WELL WORTHWHILE. IF POSSIBLE, REMOVE FROM THE FRIDGE ABOUT ONE HOUR BEFORE SERVING AS, LIKE CHEESE, THIS MOUSSE IS MUCH BETTER EATEN AT ROOM TEMPERATURE.

Remove the skin and bones from the fish and cut the flesh into small cubes (1"/2.5 cm).

Place the fish with the milk in a pan. Cover and poach the fish gently for 5 minutes. Remove the fish with a slotted spoon and place in the blender or food processor.

Chop the hard-boiled eggs and add to the fish, with the softened butter, half of the poaching milk, cayenne pepper, nutmeg and mace. Add salt and the white pepper and blend until very smooth. Place the mousse in small pots, cover with a piece of plastic film or aluminium foil and allow to set in the refrigerator overnight.

Remove from the refrigerator and dip into hot water for 5 seconds and invert on to serving plates.

Serve in very small portions with hot toast fingers and lemon wedges.

~

Stuffed Mushrooms

SERVES 4

4 extra large mushrooms
3 oz (75 g) butter
½ teaspoon oil
1 onion, very finely chopped
3 rashers back bacon, de-rinded
  and finely chopped
salt and freshly ground black
  pepper
Worcestershire sauce
zest of 1 lemon
juice of ½ lemon
3 oz (75 g) granary
  breadcrumbs
1 tablespoon chopped parsley

A WELL KNOWN LADY WRITER ONCE REMARKED – 'LIFE'S TOO SHORT TO STUFF A MUSHROOM' – WHICH HAS ALWAYS MADE ME SMILE, BUT IN TRUTH THE APPRECIATION ACCORDED TO THIS RECIPE HAS ALWAYS MADE THE EFFORT VERY WELL WORTHWHILE.

Wipe the mushrooms carefully, and remove their stalks.

Generously butter a gratin dish and stand the mushrooms top side down on the base of the dish.

In a pan heat 2 oz (50 g) of the butter with the oil and gently fry the onion with the bacon until the onion is softened. Season with salt and pepper and a dash of Worcestershire sauce, to taste. Sprinkle the lemon zest and juice into the pan, followed by the breadcrumbs. Stir the mixture gently allowing the breadcrumbs to absorb all the juices in the pan. Sprinkle on a generous tablespoon of chopped parsley and stir everything together well.

Spoon a quarter of the mixture into each mushroom cap, and top with a knob of butter.

Cover and bake in the oven at 350°F-180°C-Gas Mark 4 for 30 minutes, then remove the cover and return to the oven for a further 5 minutes.

~

Tomato Rochelle

SERVES 4

8 medium tomatoes, sliced
8 oz (225 g) goat's cheese or
* soft cream cheese*
4 tablespoons oil
4 teaspoons wine vinegar, red
* or white*
salt and freshly ground black
* pepper*
8 fresh basil leaves, shredded or
* chives, snipped*

THIS IS MY OWN PERSONAL FAVOURITE EITHER AS A FIRST COURSE OR LIGHT LUNCH, ESPECIALLY IN SUMMER WHEN FRESH BASIL LEAVES ARE AVAILABLE. I FOUND THIS RECIPE IN LA ROCHELLE, WHERE MY HOSTESS HAD ACTUALLY STUFFED THE TOMATOES WITH GOAT'S CHEESE. HERE I HAVE SIMPLIFIED THE PREPARATION, ALTHOUGH THIS DOESN'T IN ANY WAY DETRACT FROM ITS WONDERFUL DIRECT FRESHNESS AND APPEAL. IF YOU DON'T LIKE GOAT'S CHEESE THEN USE SOFT CREAM CHEESE. IF YOU CAN'T GET FRESH BASIL, THEN SUBSTITUTE A LITTLE CHOPPED PARSLEY MIXED WITH JUST A LITTLE CHOPPED TARRAGON. PLEASE, NEVER USE DRIED BASIL, IT'S NOT AS NICE.

Allow two sliced tomatoes per person. Arrange the slices overlapping across the plate, and top each portion with a quarter of the cheese, placing teaspoon sized amounts along the tomatoes.

Dress each portion with a quarter of the oil and vinegar, and season with salt and pepper.

Sprinkle the fresh, shredded basil or chives on top.

Serve with fresh crusty bread (preferably French). It's a must.

~

VEGETARIAN

Broccoli and Swiss Cheese Quiche

SERVES 4

for the pastry
4 oz (110 g) plain flour
pinch of salt
1 oz (25 g) margarine
1 oz (25 g) lard
cold water to mix (about 2
    tablespoons/30 ml)

for the filling
2 oz (50 g) butter
1 medium onion, chopped
1 lb (450 g) broccoli
2 eggs, beaten
5 fl oz (150 ml) single cream
6 fl oz (175 ml) milk
salt and pepper
8 oz (225 g) Swiss cheese,
    grated

WHEN I SAY SWISS CHEESE I MEAN OF COURSE EITHER EMMENTHAL, WITH ITS MELLOW, LIGHTLY RICH NUTTINESS, OR GRUYÈRE, WHICH HAS A FRUITIER SLIGHTLY SALTIER TANG. A FEW COUNTRIES HAVE TRIED TO COPY THEM BUT ONLY BUY THE GENUINE SWISS PRODUCT. TOGETHER THEY ARE TWO OF THE GREATEST CHEESES IN THE WORLD AND COOK BEAUTIFULLY.

First make the pastry. Mix the flour and salt in a basin and rub in the fats. Using a knife to cut and stir, mix with a little cold water to form a stiff dough. Wrap well and chill in the fridge for 30 minutes.

Preheat the oven to 350°F 180°C-Gas Mark 4. Roll out the pastry and line an 8″ (20 cm) metal flan case. Prick all over with a fork and cover with greaseproof paper, add baking beans and bake 'blind' for 12 minutes. Remove the paper and beans and return the case to the oven for a further 5 minutes. Allow to cool.

Increase the oven temperature to 375°F-190°C-Gas Mark 5.

To prepare the filling, melt the butter and gently fry the chopped onion until soft. Trim the broccoli of any thick stalks and add the florets to the pan and stir with the onions, mixing them together well. Cook gently for a further 2-3 minutes. Fill the quiche crust with the vegetable mixture.

In a bowl mix together the eggs, cream, milk, salt and pepper and pour over the vegetables. Cover the top completely with the grated cheese and bake in the oven for 30-40 minutes until a clean knife blade inserted in the centre of the quiche comes out dry.

Cool for 10 minutes before serving.

~

Brussels Sprouts with Carrot Sauce

1 lb (450 g) Brussels sprouts
½ cauliflower, in florets
small can whole, peeled
  chestnuts, rinsed and drained
  or 6 oz (175 g) fresh peeled
  chestnuts
1 oz (25 g) butter
1 oz (25 g) flour
¾ pint (425 ml) milk
3 oz (75 g) Cheddar cheese,
  grated
½ teaspoon dry mustard
  powder
salt and freshly ground black
  pepper
3 carrots, peeled and grated

WHEN I FIRST PRESENTED THIS ON TELEVISION I DIDN'T REALLY EXPECT MUCH INTEREST FROM THE STUDIO CREW AFTER THE PROGRAMME. I WAS WRONG, IN A VERY SHORT WHILE THERE WASN'T A SINGLE SPROUT LEFT – I WISH YOU THE SAME SUCCESS.

Trim the sprouts and break the cauliflower into florets. Steam them both over a pan of boiling water until just tender, but still retaining some crispness. Refresh them under cold running water. Arrange the sprouts and cauliflower with the chestnuts in the base of a well buttered ovenproof dish.

Melt the butter in a saucepan. Stir in the flour and cook for 30 seconds. Gradually add the milk, stirring continuously. Add the grated cheese, mustard powder, salt and pepper to the pan and continue stirring until the cheese is completely melted. Finally add the grated carrot and then pour the sauce over the vegetables and chestnuts.

Cook in the oven 350°F-180°C-Gas Mark 4 for 15 minutes until the top is golden brown.

This dish can be assembled up to 8 hours in advance. Just cover and keep in the fridge. Cook for 15 minutes as above before serving.

∼

Burgundy Vegetable Casserole

SERVES 4

8 oz (225 g) carrots
8 oz (225 g) onions
1 lb (450 g) potatoes
1 oz (25 g) butter
1 tablespoon oil
1 tablespoon soft brown sugar
4 oz (110 g) button mushrooms
1 tablespoon flour
¼ pint (150 ml) red wine
¼ pint (150 ml) vegetable stock
2 teaspoons tomato purée
1 bay leaf
salt and pepper
4 oz (110 g) Cheddar cheese, cubed
chopped parsley to garnish

I SUPPOSE ANOTHER WAY OF DESCRIBING THIS DISH MIGHT BE 'VEGE-TARIAN BOEUF BOURGUIGNONNE'. EITHER WAY IT'S SPLENDID AND THE MELTED CHEDDAR CUBES MAKE A LOVELY ADDITION.

Preheat the oven to 375°F-190°C-Gas Mark 5.

Peel and slice the carrots. Peel the onions and potatoes and cut both into chunks.

Melt the butter with the oil in a flameproof casserole and add the carrots, onions, potatoes and sugar, and brown gently. Add the mushrooms and continue to cook for another minute. Stir in the flour and then add the wine, stock, tomato purée, bay leaf and seasoning. Cover the casserole and cook in the oven for about 1 hour.

Ten minutes before the end of the cooking time, add the cheese and return to the oven to complete the cooking. Remove the bay leaf, check the seasoning and garnish with chopped parsley.

~

Cauliflower Casserole

SERVES 4

1 cauliflower, cut in florets
8 oz (225 g) calabrese or broccoli, cut in florets
½ pint (275 ml) low fat yoghurt
2 tablespoons wholewheat flour
8 oz (225 g) cottage cheese
salt and freshly ground black pepper
pinch of cayenne pepper
1 oz (25 g) margarine
2 oz (50 g) Edam cheese, grated
4 oz (110 g) rolled porridge oats
1 oz (25 g) sunflower seeds

I'VE ALWAYS HAD A SOFT SPOT FOR CAULIFLOWER – WHETHER BROKEN RAW INTO FLORETS AS AN IDEAL PARTY DIP SAMPLER, LIGHTLY COOKED AND SMOTHERED IN CREAMY, CHEESE SAUCE, OR EVEN IN MY FAVOURITE SUPER SAUCE (PAGE 118). FOR A MAIN MEAL, PARTNERED BY CONTRASTING BROCCOLI, THIS IS WELL WORTH TRY-ING.

Partly cook the cauliflower and broccoli florets in boiling salted water for 4-5 minutes until they are about half cooked, then drain.

Pour the yoghurt into a saucepan and then stir in the flour. Mix together over a low heat, stirring all the time until simmering. Re-move from the heat and stir in the cottage cheese, and season to taste with salt, black and cayenne peppers.

Arrange the vegetables in a buttered casserole and pour over the sauce.

In a bowl mix together the margarine, grated cheese, oats and sunflower seeds, and sprinkle this mixture over the dish. Cook the casserole, uncovered, in a fairly hot oven – 400°F-200°C-Gas Mark 6 – for 30-35 minutes until bubbling. Serve hot.

Minestrone Soup (page 3) and *Tomato Rochelle* (page 13).

Cheese and Sweetcorn Flan

THE TITLE HERE TELLS YOU ALL YOU NEED TO KNOW AND IF YOU HAVE HUNGRY YOUNG MOUTHS TO FILL THERE'S EVERY POSSIBILITY THAT THIS WILL BECOME A FIRM FAMILY FAVOURITE.

SERVES 4

for the pastry
6 oz (175 g) plain flour
½ teaspoon salt
1½ oz (40 g) margarine
1½ oz (40 g) lard
cold water to mix (about 2 tablespoons (30 ml))

for the filling
1 medium onion
12 oz (350 g) can sweetcorn with peppers
1 oz (25 g) butter
4 oz (110 g) Cheddar cheese
2 teaspoons mixed herbs
2 eggs
¼ pint (150 ml) milk
½ teaspoon salt
¼ teaspoon ground black pepper
chopped parsley to garnish

Sieve the flour and salt into a bowl. Add the margarine and lard cut into pieces and rub them into the flour until the mixture resembles fine breadcrumbs. Stir in enough cold water to form a dough.

Roll out the pastry on a lightly floured board to a thickness of about ¼" (5 mm) and use it to line a greased 8" (20 cm) flan dish.

To prepare the filling, chop the onion finely and drain the sweetcorn. Melt the butter in a pan and fry the onion and sweetcorn with peppers together until they are soft and just beginning to colour. Grate the cheese and place it in the bottom of the pastry case. Sprinkle the mixed herbs over the cheese and cover with the onion and sweetcorn mixture. Beat the eggs with the milk, salt and ground pepper. Pour the mixture carefully over the filling in the pastry case. Place the dish on a flat baking sheet and cook in the oven at 400°F-200°C-Gas Mark 6 for 35-40 minutes, or until the flan is firm, well risen and golden.

Delicious served hot or cold and sprinkled with chopped parsley.

~

Mussels with Tomatoes and Leeks (page 36) and Mushrooms Stuffed with Nutty Rice (page 20).

Mushrooms Stuffed with Nutty Rice

SERVES 4

8 oz (225 g) open mushrooms
1 tablespoon sunflower oil
1 onion, finely chopped
1 small carrot, grated
1 clove garlic, crushed
4 oz (110 g) cooked brown rice
1 tablespoon chopped parsley
2 oz (50 g) chopped nuts
salt and freshly ground black pepper
1 oz (25 g) fresh breadcrumbs
1 oz (25 g) Parmesan cheese, grated
grated zest of 1 lemon

THIS ALTERNATIVE STUFFED MUSHROOM RECIPE FEATURES BROWN RICE WHICH, DESPITE ITS LONGER COOKING TIME (ABOUT 40 MINUTES), MANY PEOPLE PREFER FOR ITS NUTTIER FLAVOUR.

Wipe the mushrooms and remove their stalks. Chop the stalks finely and keep to one side. Place the mushroom caps dark side up, in a greased gratin dish.

In a pan heat the oil and gently cook the onion, carrot and finely chopped mushroom stalks until soft. Add the garlic and mix well. Transfer to a bowl. When the mixture has cooled a little add the cooked rice, parsley and nuts. Mix well again and season with salt and pepper.

Fill the mushrooms with the mixture, patting gently into shape.

In a bowl mix together the breadcrumbs, Parmesan cheese and the lemon zest. Sprinkle this mixture over the mushroom tops and bake in the oven at 350°F-180°C-Gas Mark 4 for about 30 minutes, or until nicely browned.

~

Pine and Pepper Loaf

SERVES 4

4 oz (110 g) pine kernels
2 oz (50 g) cashew nuts
2 oz (50 g) wholemeal breadcrumbs
2 oz (50 g) ground almonds
2 sticks celery, chopped
1 medium onion, chopped
1 red pepper
1 green pepper
2 tablespoons oil
3 eggs, beaten
¼ pint (150 ml) milk
salt and pepper
2 oz (50 g) melted butter

WE'RE QUITE A LONG WAY AWAY FROM THE FAMED 'NUT CUTLET' AND WITH THREE OF THE WORLD'S TOP NUTS INVOLVED, THIS IS CERTAINLY A HIGH QUALITY, MEAT-FREE BAKE. IDEAL FOR A SPECIAL VEGETARIAN OCCASION.

Put the pine kernels into a large bowl with the cashew nuts, breadcrumbs and ground almonds and mix them all well together.

Chop the celery and onion finely, and core, de-seed and finely chop the red and green peppers. Heat the oil in a large pan and gently fry the celery, onion and peppers until soft.

Transfer to the bowl with the nuts and mix everything together gently. Add the beaten eggs to the bowl with the milk and the melted butter. Season well with salt and pepper.

Put the mixture into a greased or non-stick 2 lb (900 g) loaf tin and bake in the oven at 375°F-190°C-Gas Mark 5 for 40-50 minutes until brown on top and firm to the touch. Allow to cool in the tin before turning out.

Accompany with a good tomato sauce (see page 118).

Squash Casserole

SERVES 4

1 large marrow
3 oz (75 g) butter
1 large onion, chopped
2 cloves garlic, crushed
salt
1 small green pepper
1 small red pepper
2 eggs
8 fl oz (225 ml) natural yoghurt
4 oz (110 g) feta cheese
black pepper and paprika
2 oz (50 g) sunflower seeds

ON ITS OWN THE MARROW DEFINITELY LACKS PERSONALITY, WHICH IS WHY I THINK THIS CASSEROLE IDEA WILL BE WELCOMED AS A VERY ENJOYABLE ADDITION TO THE MORE USUAL STUFFED MARROW RECIPES.

Peel the marrow, remove the seeds and poach the flesh in boiling salted water until tender. Remove from the water with a slotted spoon to a large bowl and mash well.

Melt the butter in a pan and fry the onion and garlic together with a pinch of salt until they are soft. Meanwhile de-seed and chop the red and green peppers and add to the pan. Continue to cook with the onion for a minute or two.

In a bowl beat the eggs and the yoghurt together, and when well mixed, crumble the feta cheese into the bowl. Then add the cooked onion and peppers mixture, the mashed marrow flesh and mix everything well. Season with salt, pepper and a little paprika.

Put the mixture into a buttered casserole dish. Smooth the top and scatter the sunflower seeds all over.

Bake in the oven at 375°F-190°C-Gas Mark 5 for about 35 minutes.

Serve either as a vegetarian main dish or as a vegetable accompaniment to meat.

~

Terrific Tart

SERVES 4

7 oz (200 g) puff pastry
3 oz (75 g) cream cheese
3 oz (75 g) blue cheese
3 oz (75 g) Camembert or Brie
½ oz (10 g) butter
1 small onion, finely chopped
5 tablespoons single cream
3 eggs
salt and pepper

IT IS!

Preheat the oven to 400°F-200°C-Gas Mark 6.

Roll out the pastry and line a 9″ (23 cm) flan tin. Prick the pastry with a fork, cover with greaseproof paper, add baking beans and bake 'blind' for 10 minutes. Remove from the oven, take out the paper and beans and leave to cool slightly.

Meanwhile put the three cheeses into a bowl and mash them with the butter and the chopped onion. Add the cream with the whole eggs, season to taste, and beat everything together well.

Pour the mixture into the flan case and bake in the oven at the same temperature for about 35 minutes, until set. Delicious eaten hot or cold.

Vegetarian Shepherd's Pie

6 oz (175 g) whole brown or
   green lentils
4 oz (110 g) green or yellow
   split peas
1 pint (570 ml) hot water
2 oz (50 g) butter
1 medium onion, chopped
2 carrots, peeled and chopped
2 sticks celery, chopped
½ green pepper, de-seeded and
   chopped
1 clove garlic, crushed
1 tablespoon mixed fresh herbs
   or 2 teaspoons dried mixed
   herbs
2 pinches ground mace
¼ teaspoon cayenne pepper
salt and freshly ground black
   pepper
8 oz (225 g) tomatoes

for the topping
1½ lb (700 g) potatoes
3 oz (75 g) butter
1 small onion, chopped
2 tablespoons single cream
3 oz (75 g) Cheddar cheese,
   grated
salt and pepper

VEGETARIANS TO ME ARE PEOPLE WHO CARE ABOUT WHAT THEY EAT AND CONSEQUENTLY TAKE A LOT MORE TROUBLE ABOUT THEIR NOURISHMENT THAN MANY. THIS RECIPE WILL, I HOPE, PROVE USEFUL TO ANYONE IN NEED OF A MEATLESS MEAL. IT'S PACKED WITH GOODNESS AND IT'S VERY FILLING.

Begin by washing the lentils and split peas and then put them in a saucepan with the hot water and simmer gently, covered, for about 45-60 minutes or until the peas and lentils have absorbed the water and are soft.

Preheat the oven to 375°F-190°C-Gas Mark 5.

Meanwhile melt the butter in a frying pan and add the onion, carrots, celery, green pepper and garlic. Cook gently until softened. Remove from the heat and mash a little before adding the vegetables to the cooked lentil mixture. Stir in the fresh herbs (or dried, if using), mace, salt and peppers. Spoon the mixture into a large, buttered pie dish (3 pint/1.75 litre).

Peel the tomatoes by covering them with boiling water for about 30 seconds. Remove and slip off the skins under the cold water tap. Slice the flesh and arrange the tomatoes over the top of the pie.

To prepare the topping, peel the potatoes and cook them in boiling water until tender. Then drain and mash with 2 oz (50 g) of the butter. Melt the remaining 1 oz (25 g) of butter in a pan and soften the onion gently. Add the onion to the mashed potatoes with the cream and the grated cheese and mix together well. Season to taste and then spread on top of the ingredients in the pie dish.

Bake in the oven for about 20 minutes until the top is lightly browned.

~

Wholewheat Pizza

WE TAKE IT FOR GRANTED NOW, OF COURSE, BUT WHO WOULD HAVE GUESSED THAT A SIMPLE NEAPOLITAN DOUGH WOULD ACHIEVE SUCH FAME AND POPULARITY WITH MILLIONS OF FANS ALL OVER THE GLOBE? FOR HOME BAKERS HERE'S A TASTY WHOLEWHEAT VERSION MADE IN A SWISS ROLL TRAY.

SERVES 4

for the base
½ oz (10 g) yeast
1 tablespoon soya flour
¼ pint (150 ml) warm water
8 oz (225 g) wholewheat flour
pinch of salt
1 dessertspoon oil

for the topping
2 tablespoons olive oil
1 lb (450 g) onions, finely
   chopped
2 cloves garlic, crushed
2 teaspoons oregano
2 tablespoons tomato purée
salt and pepper
8 oz (225 g) Mozzarella cheese,
   sliced
1 green pepper, de-seeded and
   sliced
4 tomatoes, sliced
16 black olives

In a small bowl mix together the yeast, soya flour and warm water. Leave for 5 minutes.

Mix together the wholewheat flour and salt, and pour over the yeast mixture. Add the oil, stir well and then knead together to form a smooth dough. Leave to rest in a clean bowl for 10-20 minutes.

Roll out to fit a swiss roll tray. Prick all over with a fork and leave again for 15 minutes. Then bake in the oven at 425°F-220°C-Gas Mark 7 for just 4 minutes. Remove from the oven and make the topping.

Heat the oil and add the onions and garlic and cook gently for 20 minutes. Add the oregano, tomato purée and a little water. Allow the mixture to stew for another 5-10 minutes until everything is very soft. Season well. Spoon the topping over the base and cover with the slices of Mozzarella cheese. Arrange the green pepper slices, the tomatoes and olives all over the top of the pizza and bake in the oven (425°F-220°C-Gas Mark 7) for 15-20 minutes or until the cheese has melted and is golden brown.

~

A lot has been written and said about fish in recent times, especially concerning health, to which I would fervently add that if you are fortunate enough to have one, please support your local fishmonger. If you do not, they will probably have to give up, as many already have, and we shall all be the poorer for their departure.

F I S H

Bacon and Prawn Creole

SERVES 4

8 oz (225 g) unsmoked bacon
2 tablespoons butter
2 oz (50 g) onion, thinly sliced
1 chilli pepper, de-seeded and
    chopped
1 clove garlic, crushed
2 oz (50 g) sliced peppers, red
    or green
14 oz (400 g) can tomatoes,
    liquidised
4 fl oz (110 ml) double cream
8 oz (225 g) prawns, peeled
salt and pepper
8 oz (225 g) long-grain rice
spring onions and chopped
    parsley to garnish

FROM THE AMERICAN SOUTH THIS IS A LIVELY AND COLOURFUL COM-
BINATION WHICH DOESN'T TAKE ALL DAY TO PREPARE. IDEAL FOR
ENTERTAINING.

Cut the bacon into 2″ (5 cm) strips. Heat the butter in a saucepan
and toss the bacon, onion, chilli pepper and garlic together over a
moderate heat for a couple of minutes. Then add the sliced red
and green peppers and the puréed tomatoes. Bring to the boil and
then stir in the cream and the prawns.

Simmer gently for 5 minutes, season with salt and pepper and
serve on a bed of boiled rice, garnished with the chopped spring
onions.

Sprinkle with chopped parsley before serving.

~

Baked Haddock with Mustard Mayonnaise

SERVES 4

1½ lb (700 g) fresh haddock
    fillets
1 oz (25 g) butter
salt
1 teaspoon English mustard
    powder
4 fl oz (110 ml) mayonnaise
¼ onion, finely chopped
1 teaspoon fresh thyme, finely
    chopped
1 teaspoon lemon juice
freshly ground pepper

ONE OF MY FAVOURITE FISH, THE FIRM FLESHED HADDOCK RESPONDS
VERY WELL TO A VARIETY OF TREATMENTS. THIS MUSTARD MAYON-
NAISE IS PARTICULARLY TASTY.

Preheat the oven to 350°F-180°C-Gas Mark 4.

Butter a baking dish and place the fish fillets in the base.
Sprinkle them with salt.

Make the mustard by mixing with a little water in the usual way
and allow to stand for 10 minutes.

When ready, in a bowl mix together the mustard, mayonnaise,
finely chopped onion, thyme, lemon juice and freshly ground
black pepper. Spread this mixture over the fish fillets and bake in
the oven for 25 minutes or until the fish is flaky and the sauce is
light golden brown.

~

Brittany Cod

SERVES 4

1½ lb (700 g) fresh cod fillet
1½ lb (700 g) potatoes, peeled
  and sliced
3 oz (75 g) butter
1 large onion, sliced
oil
8 oz (225 g) bacon slices
salt and freshly ground black
  pepper
8 fl oz (225 ml) cream

THIS MAY BE NEW TO YOU BUT THE COD, BACON AND POTATO COM-
BINATION WORKS VERY WELL AND HAS DONE SO FOR A VERY LONG
TIME FOR THE INHABITANTS OF NORTH-WEST FRANCE.

Preheat the oven to 400°F-200°C-Gas Mark 6.

Cut the cod fillet into medium-sized pieces. Peel the potatoes
and then slice them thinly.

Melt 2 oz (50 g) of the butter in a pan and cook the chopped
onion gently until soft.

Oil a deep ovenproof dish. Cover the bottom of the dish with
half the bacon slices, half the cooked onion and half of the potato
slices. Place the fish pieces on top. Season well with salt and pepper. Cover the fish with the rest of the bacon slices, onion and
potatoes. Season well and pour the cream over the top.

Dot with the remaining 1 oz (25 g) of butter and cook in the oven
for about 1 hour.

Best served straight from the dish.

~

Cod and Camembert

SERVES 4

4 cod fillets
juice of ½ lemon
2 tablespoons flour
salt
2 oz (50 g) butter
2 red or green peppers
2 rashers of bacon, cut into thin
  strips
6 oz (175 g) Camembert, cut
  into cubes
1 small glass white wine
2 tablespoons flaked almonds
grated Parmesan cheese

SURPRISINGLY, SIMPLE EVERYDAY COD FILLET IS THE BASIS FOR THIS
EYE-CATCHING DISH WHOSE TASTE FULLY LIVES UP TO ITS GOOD
LOOKS.

Preheat the oven to 375°F-190°C-Gas Mark 5.

Wash the cod fillets, drain and pat dry. Sprinkle the fish with
the lemon juice and dust with flour and salt.

Heat the butter in a frying pan and fry the cod fillets until just
brown on both sides. Remove the fish and lay in a shallow ovenproof dish.

De-seed the peppers and cut into rings. Put the pepper rings,
bacon and Camembert on top of the cod fillets.

Pour over the white wine and sprinkle with the flaked almonds
and grated Parmesan cheese. Dot a little butter on the top and
bake in the oven until golden brown.

Serve with parsley potatoes and a green salad.

Coriander Cod Crumble

SERVES 4

*4 × 6 oz (175 g) cod or haddock
  fillets, skinned*
butter
*salt and freshly ground black
  pepper*
*14 oz (400 g) can chopped
  tomatoes*
*2 teaspoons fresh oregano or
  marjoram, chopped or 1
  teaspoon dried*
2 oz (50 g) butter
1 oz (25 g) blue cheese
*3 oz (75g) wholemeal plain
  flour*
2 oz (50 g) rolled oats
1 teaspoon ground coriander
1 teaspoon chilli powder
*6 oz (175 g) mature Cheddar
  cheese, grated*

THE SLIGHT NOTE OF BURNT ORANGE FROM THE CORIANDER
TOGETHER WITH THE OATS, CHILLI AND TWO CHEESES CREATES A
WONDERFUL TOPPING FOR THE TOMATO AND HERB FLAVOURED FISH.

Arrange the fish portions in a buttered, shallow ovenproof dish.
Season with salt and pepper and pour the tomatoes over the top.
Sprinkle with oregano or marjoram.

In a bowl blend together the 2 oz (50 g) butter with the 1 oz (25 g)
blue cheese. Add the flour and work the butter mixture with the
flour by rubbing it through the fingertips until the mixture resembles breadcrumbs. Then stir in the oats, coriander, chilli and
grated Cheddar cheese.

Spoon the crumble mixture over the top of the fish and tomatoes.

Bake in the oven at 375°F-190°C-Gas Mark 5 for 30-40 minutes
until the topping is golden and crisp.

~

Crab Quiche

SERVES 4

for the pastry
4 oz (110 g) plain flour
pinch of salt
1 oz (25 g) lard
1 oz (25 g) margarine
cold water to mix

for the filling
3 oz (75 g) onion or shallot
2 oz (50 g) butter
1-2 cloves garlic, crushed
6 oz (175 g) crabmeat
2 egg yolks
4 fl oz (110 ml) double cream
salt and pepper
pinch of freshly grated nutmeg
1 tablespoon parsley, chopped

THIS IS A TRULY SUPERB RECIPE WITH AN ADDITIONAL BONUS; THE CRABMEAT CAN BE SUBSTITUTED, ACCORDING TO SEASON OR FANCY, BY AN EQUAL WEIGHT OF SALMON, SMOKED HADDOCK, ASPARAGUS, PRAWNS, LEEKS OR MUSHROOMS. IT CAN BE EATEN COLD, BUT FOR MAXIMUM PLEASURE I PREFER IT STILL WARM FROM THE OVEN.

To make the pastry sift the flour and salt into a bowl. Add the fats cut into small pieces and rub in with the fingertips until the mixture resembles breadcrumbs. Using a knife mix in a little cold water gradually to form a stiff dough.

Chill for 20 minutes before rolling out.

Use the pastry to line a greased, loose-bottomed 7" (18 cm) flan tin. Prick the base of the pastry and line with paper and baking beans and bake 'blind' on the centre shelf at 350°F-180°C-Gas Mark 4 for about 10 minutes. Remove the paper and beans and return the pastry case to the oven for a further 5 minutes.

Now for the filling. Finely chop the onion or shallot. Melt the butter in a pan and soften the onion with the garlic. When soft but not brown remove from the heat and allow to cool. Spread the mixture over the bottom of the flan case. Top with the flaked crabmeat or other chosen filling.

In a bowl beat together gently the egg yolks with the double cream. Season with salt, pepper and nutmeg. Fold in the chopped parsley.

Pour this mixture over the filling and bake on a baking tray at 375°F-190°C-Gas Mark 5 for about 25-30 minutes until just set and light brown on top.

~

Double Delight

SERVES 4

1¼ lb (550 g) cod fillet
8 oz (225 g) smoked haddock
  fillet
1½ pints (850 ml) fish or
  chicken stock
1 onion, sliced
1 clove garlic, crushed
salt and pepper
3 whole cloves
2 oz (50 g) butter
1 dessertspoon flour
5 tomatoes
2 eggs
2 oz (50 g) Parmesan cheese,
  grated
8 fl oz (225 ml) milk
chopped parsley to garnish

ANOTHER SLIGHTLY UNUSUAL COMBINATION USING BOTH FRESH AND SMOKED FISH. THE RESULT, FOLLOWING THE INITIAL COOKING IN WONDERFULLY FLAVOURED MILK, IS REALLY DELICIOUS.

Remove all skin and any bones from the fish, and cut both fish into 1″ (2.5 cm) slices.

In a saucepan place the fish with the stock, onion, garlic, salt, pepper and the whole cloves. Bring gently to the boil and simmer for 10 minutes. Remove the fish with a little of the onion, using a slotted spoon, and place in a buttered ovenproof dish. Continue to boil the cooking stock until reduced to about ½ pint (275 ml).

In another pan melt 1 oz (25 g) of the butter and stir in the flour. When they are well mixed pour on the reduced stock, stirring all the time, to make a smooth sauce. Check for seasoning and then pour the sauce over the fish.

Plunge the tomatoes into boiling water for 20 seconds. Remove and peel off their skins under the cold tap. Then slice, and layer over the top of the fish.

In a bowl beat together the eggs, with a little salt and pepper, add the grated cheese and then beat in the milk. Pour this mixture over the fish and tomatoes, and bake in the oven at 350°F-180°C-Gas Mark 4 for about 45 minutes, until golden brown on top. Sprinkle with chopped parsley and serve.

~

Favourite Fish Dish

SERVES 4

4 × 12 oz (350 g) plaice, dab or
  sole
1½ oz (40 g) flour
salt and pepper
1 tablespoon oil
4 oz (110 g) butter
12 spring onions, sliced
8 oz (225 g) cooked prawns or
  shrimps
3 tablespoons capers
juice of 2 lemons
2 tablespoons fresh herbs,
  chopped

THE CHOICE OF FISH IS UP TO YOU AND THE DELICIOUS DRESSING, WHICH COULDN'T BE SIMPLER TO PREPARE, LIFTS THE WHOLE THING INTO A CLASS OF ITS OWN.

Take one fish at a time and lightly dust with the flour, seasoned with salt and pepper.

Heat the oil with 2 oz (50 g) of the butter and gently fry the fish until slightly browned and cooked through. Remove to a heated serving dish and keep warm.

Melt 2 oz (50 g) of butter in a pan and add the spring onions, prawns or shrimps, capers, lemon juice and fresh herbs. Heat through and then spread over the cooked fish.

Serve at once.

Haddock in Curry Sauce

SERVES 4

1½ lb (700 g) haddock fillets
1½ oz (40 g) butter
2 onions, finely chopped
1 clove garlic, crushed
1 tablespoon curry powder
1 tablespoon plain flour
8 oz (225 g) tomatoes
½ pint (275 ml) fish or chicken
  stock
2 tablespoons tomato purée
¼ teaspoon fresh chopped (or
  ground) ginger
1 tablespoon lemon juice
salt and freshly ground black
  pepper
to garnish: lemon wedges and a
  sprinkle of marjoram,
  chopped

WE DON'T HAVE A GREAT FISH STEW TRADITION HERE, AS IN FRANCE AND SPAIN, AND SO IT'S EASY TO OVERLOOK A WHOLE RANGE OF QUICK TO COOK, DELICIOUS FISH CASSEROLES. THIS ONE IS ESPECIALLY NICE AND FLAVOURSOME.

Skin the haddock fillets (or ask your fishmonger to do this for you) and cut into 1" (2.5 cm) cubes.

Place the fish in a buttered ovenproof casserole.

Melt the butter in a pan and gently fry the onion and garlic together until the onion is soft but not browned.

In a small bowl mix together the curry powder and flour and sprinkle this over the onions in the pan. Cook, stirring, for 2 minutes.

Skin the tomatoes by plunging into boiling water for 20 seconds, then remove and peel skins under cold water. Chop the tomato flesh.

Remove the onion pan from the heat and stir in the chopped tomatoes, stock, tomato purée, ginger, lemon juice and salt and pepper to taste. Return to the heat and bring to the boil, stirring, then pour over the fish in the casserole. Stir gently to mix through. Cover and cook in the oven at 325°F-170°C-Gas Mark 3 for 30 minutes.

Surround with lemon wedges, sprinkle with marjoram if used, and serve with boiled rice.

~

Haddock in Cream

SERVES 4

1½ lb (700 g) haddock fillet
2 tablespoons lemon juice
1 teaspoon made mustard
½ teaspoon Worcestershire
  sauce
1 teaspoon salt
¼ teaspoon pepper
3 small onions, sliced in rings
approx 8 fl oz (225 ml) cream
paprika
chopped parsley to garnish

ANOTHER NOVEL IDEA WITH LEMON, MUSTARD, SEASONINGS AND CREAM.

Preheat the oven to 400°F-200°C-Gas Mark 6.

Rinse the haddock fillet and pat dry with kitchen towel. Place in the bottom of a well-buttered baking dish.

In a bowl mix together the lemon juice, mustard, Worcestershire sauce, salt and pepper. Pour the mixture over the fish. Scatter the thinly sliced onion rings over the top and then pour on the cream. Bake in the oven for about 30 minutes.

Just before serving dust the top of the dish with some paprika and sprinkle over some chopped parsley.

Italian Honey-baked Cod

SERVES 6

6 cod cutlets
14 oz (400 g) can tomatoes
2 tablespoons lemon juice
3 tablespoons clear honey
2 teaspoons tomato purée
2 tablespoons water
1 teaspoon oregano, chopped
salt and freshly ground black
* pepper*
1 onion, sliced in rings
1 green pepper, de-seeded and
* sliced in rings*
1 bay leaf
1½ oz (40 g) flaked almonds

QUITE AN OUTSTANDING FISH DISH IN WHICH THE SURPRISING COM-
BINATION OF INGREDIENTS RESULTS IN A MEAL TO REMEMBER.

Arrange the cod cutlets in a shallow, buttered ovenproof dish.
Drain the juice from the can of tomatoes into a bowl, and mix with
it the lemon juice, honey, tomato purée, water, oregano, salt and
pepper.

Scatter the onion and pepper rings over the fish, then add the
tomatoes with the bay leaf. Pour the honey sauce over the top.

Cover the dish and bake in the oven at 375°F-190°C-Gas Mark 5
for 25 minutes, basting the fish once or twice during that time.

After the 25 minutes, remove the cover, scatter with the flaked
almonds and return uncovered to the oven for a few minutes to
brown the nuts.

~

Kedgeree

SERVES 4

1½ lb (700 g) smoked haddock
¾ pint (425 ml) milk
1 bay leaf
4 black peppercorns
sprig of parsley
6 oz (175 g) long grain rice
3 hard-boiled eggs
6 tablespoons butter
1½ teaspoons curry paste
salt and freshly ground black
    pepper
1½ oz (40 g) butter
1½ oz (40 g) flour
6-8 tablespoons double cream
2 tablespoons lemon juice
3 tablespoons chopped parsley

ENJOYED BY GENERATIONS, PARTICULARLY AS A BREAKFAST DISH, TODAY'S EATING FASHION MAKES IT MORE SUITABLE AS A SUBSTANTIAL LUNCHEON OR EVEN SUPPER DISH. IT'S PACKED WITH GOOD THINGS AND THE SMALL HINT OF CURRY SPICES LENDS EXTRA INTEREST.

First poach the fish by placing it in a saucepan with the milk, bay leaf, peppercorns and sprig of parsley. Bring just to the boil, then reduce the heat and simmer gently for about 8 minutes. Strain the liquid from the fish and reserve. Dice or flake the fish carefully, removing any bones or skin.

Cook the rice in plenty of boiling salted water for 12 minutes, then strain, run under cold water and keep on one side. Shell the hard-boiled eggs and separate the yolks from the whites and chop the whites finely.

Melt the butter in a large pan and blend in the curry paste. Add the fish and toss over a gentle heat until thoroughly hot and golden. Add the rice to the pan and the finely chopped egg whites. Toss lightly until well mixed, taking care not to crumble the fish. Season to taste with salt and freshly ground black pepper, remove from the heat and keep hot.

In another pan melt the 1½ oz (40 g) butter and stir in the 1½ oz (40 g) flour, cook for 2 minutes and then blend in the reserved liquid from the fish, stirring constantly until the sauce thickens. Stir in the double cream and sharpen the flavour with lemon juice, salt and pepper to taste.

Fold the sauce into the rice mixture, together with the chopped parsley. When well mixed turn the kedgeree into a heated serving dish. Sieve hard-boiled egg yolks over the top and serve very hot.

~

Magnificent Mussels

SERVES 3

3 lb (1½ kg) mussels, cleaned
1 glass white wine (or cider)
sprig of parsley
½ lemon
1 onion, roughly chopped
pinch of thyme
1 bay leaf
¼ pint (150 ml) fresh milk
2 oz (50 g) butter
1 teaspoon oil
1 onion, very finely chopped
1 large carrot, grated
1½ tablespoons flour
1 teaspoon curry powder
¼ teaspoon ground nutmeg
2 tablespoons chopped parsley

DESPITE THEIR INCREASING POPULARITY THERE ARE STILL A VAST NUMBER OF PEOPLE WHO HAVE NEVER TASTED THIS CHEAP, NOURISHING AND DELIGHTFUL SHELLFISH, AND IT IS A REAL SHAME. MOST OF US WHO HAVE TASTED MUSSELS PROBABLY DID SO FIRST AS MOULES MARINIÈRE, THAT GREAT AND SIMPLE CLASSIC FRENCH DISH. THE FOLLOWING THREE RECIPES ARE RATHER MORE ADVENTUROUS AND I PROMISE THAT ANY ONE OF THESE WILL BE MET WITH DELIGHTFUL APPRECIATION.

FIRST, A NOTE ON PREPARING MUSSELS. DISCARD ANY MUSSELS WHICH REFUSE TO CLOSE WITH A SLIGHT PRESSURE FROM THE FINGERS, AS THEY ARE DEAD. WASH THE MUSSELS UNDER RUNNING WATER AND WITH A SHARP KNIFE SCRAPE OFF ANY GRIT, LUMPS ETC. ALSO PULL AWAY ANY BITS OF WEED WHICH MAY BE TRAPPED IN THE SHELL. RINSE WELL IN COLD WATER AND PROCEED WITH THE RECIPE.

Place the cleaned mussels in a large saucepan together with the wine, sprig of parsley, lemon, roughly chopped onion, pinch of thyme and the bay leaf.

Cover and cook over a high heat until all the mussels have opened, 3-5 minutes, shaking the pan occasionally during that time. Discard any mussels that have not opened.

Strain off ½ pint (275 ml) of the cooking liquid into a jug and make it up to ¾ pint (425 ml) with the fresh milk. Remove and discard one shell from each mussel, and place the mussels in a large bowl and keep warm.

To make the sauce begin by melting the butter and oil in a pan and add the finely chopped onion with the grated carrot and cook together gently until soft. Add the flour and curry powder with the nutmeg to the pan and stir until a thick paste is achieved. Remove the pan from the heat and add a little of the stock, stirring all the time. When that has blended in add a little more and repeat until all the stock has been added. Return to the heat and allow to cook very gently stirring occasionally for 10-15 minutes. Add the mussels mixing them into the sauce and when thoroughly hot throw on the chopped parsley and serve.

~

Master's Mussels

4 lb (2 kg) mussels
½ pint (275 ml) dry white wine
1 tablespoon Pernod (optional)
salt and pepper
2 oz (50 g) butter
1 onion, finely chopped
1 clove garlic, crushed
1 tablespoon flour
pinch of saffron, infused in a
    little water
2 egg yolks
5 fl oz (150 ml) double cream

Scrub the mussels, trim the beards and discard any which aren't tightly shut. Place the mussels in a large saucepan with the wine (and Pernod, if using) and salt and pepper. Cover the pot with a lid and put on a high heat for 5 minutes. Shake the saucepan a couple of times during cooking. Then remove the mussels from the liquid with a slotted spoon and keep in a warm place. (Discard any mussels that have not opened.)

Strain off the cooking liquid into a jug. You should have about 1 pint (570 ml).

Melt 2 oz (50 g) butter in a pan and soften the finely chopped onion with the garlic over a gentle heat. Stir in the flour and then slowly add the reserved mussel and wine liquor and the saffron water, stirring constantly until well blended together. Allow this sauce to cook gently for 5-10 minutes.

When the sauce is ready, remove it from the heat. Mix together the two egg yolks and the double cream and stir gently into the sauce. Return to the heat but do not allow to boil.

When heated through pour the sauce over the mussels and serve immediately with French bread.

~

Mussels with Tomatoes and Leeks

SERVES 4

3-4 lb (1-2 kg) mussels
1 lb (450 g) tomatoes
3 oz (75 g) butter
1 lb (450 g) leeks, sliced thinly
salt and freshly ground pepper
2 cloves garlic, crushed
grated zest of 1 small lemon
½ pint (275 ml) dry white wine
bay leaf
1 tablespoon flour
2 tablespoons chopped parsley

Scrub the mussels well, trim the beards and scrape off any barnacles. Discard any which aren't tightly shut.

Put the tomatoes in a bowl. Pour over boiling water to just cover. Leave them for 30 seconds, then drain and slip off their skins. Chop the flesh roughly. Put on one side.

Melt 2 oz (50 g) of the butter in a large saucepan and add the sliced leeks, seasoning and garlic and cook gently for 2-3 minutes. Stir in the lemon zest, wine and bay leaf. Now add the mussels and bring quickly to the boil. Cover and cook on a high heat for about 4 minutes, giving the pot an occasional good shake.

When all the mussels are open – discard any which are still closed – remove them to a large serving dish. Discard the bay leaf.

Cream together the remaining butter and the flour and add it in little knobs to the cooking liquid. Bring to the boil and stir until fully absorbed. Reduce the heat and stir in the roughly chopped tomatoes and the parsley and cook for a further minute. Pour the sauce over the mussels and serve at once with warm crusty bread.

~

Nutty Fish Fillets

SERVES 4

1½ lb (700 g) cod or haddock
*   fillets*
salt and pepper
juice of ½ lemon
4 oz (110 g) nuts, finely
*   chopped*
4 oz (110 g) Cheddar cheese,
*   grated*
2 dessertspoons sherry
3 fl oz (75 ml) milk
3 oz (75 g) fresh breadcrumbs
¼ teaspoon grated nutmeg
2 oz (50 g) butter

THE CRUNCHY, NUTTY CHEESE BAKED TOPPING HERE COMPLEMENTS PERFECTLY THE YIELDING TENDERNESS OF THE FISH.

Preheat the oven to 400°F-200°C-Gas Mark 6.

Place the fish fillets in a shallow, buttered ovenproof dish. Season with salt, pepper and the lemon juice.

In a bowl bind together the chopped nuts with the cheese, sherry and milk. When well mixed spread over the top of the fish.

Place the breadcrumbs in another bowl and season them with salt, pepper and nutmeg, then sprinkle over the top of the dish.

Dot the top with butter and bake in the preheated oven for 30 minutes.

~

Oven-fried Plaice à la Nicoise

SERVES 4-6

8 oz (225 g) dry breadcrumbs
2-4 tablespoons chopped parsley
2 cloves garlic, finely chopped
freshly grated peel ½ lemon
¼ teaspoon fresh thyme
1 level tablespoon salt
½ pint (275 ml) milk
4-6 plaice, filleted
4 tablespoons butter
*paprika and lemon wedges to
    garnish*

'FISH IS FINE ANY TIME' AND THIS IS A RECIPE YOU WILL WANT TO TRY
AGAIN AND AGAIN.

Preheat the oven to 425°F-220°C-Gas Mark 7.

In a bowl mix together the breadcrumbs, chopped parsley, garlic, grated lemon peel and thyme. In a separate bowl add the salt and milk.

Take each plaice fillet and dip first in the milk and then coat with the breadcrumb mixture. Arrange the fillets in a well-buttered baking dish. Melt the butter in a saucepan and pour over the fillets.

Place the dish on the top shelf of the oven and cook for about 12 minutes. Garnish with paprika and lemon wedges and serve immediately.

~

Party Prawns

THIS IS JUST THE THING FOR A PARTY BUFFET TABLE. IN STYLE THERE IS A SLIGHT RESEMBLANCE TO THE WELL KNOWN CORONATION CHICKEN, BUT I THINK THIS IS FAR NICER AND YOU CAN, IF YOU WISH, SUBSTITUTE A SIMILAR WEIGHT OF DICED COOKED CHICKEN FOR THE PRAWNS. EITHER WAY, IT'S DELICIOUS.

SERVES 6

12 oz (350 g) uncooked rice,
   white or brown
5 tablespoons French dressing
2 oz (50 g) sultanas
1½ lb (700 g) peeled prawns,
   defrosted

for the sauce
2 tablespoons oil
1 onion, finely chopped
1 apple, cored and chopped
2 teaspoons flour
1 rounded tablespoon curry
   powder
2 tablespoons mango chutney
15 oz (425 g) can tomatoes

for the mayonnaise
6 tablespoons mayonnaise
juice of ½ lemon
salt and black pepper
dash of Tabasco
chives and parsley to garnish

First cook the rice according to type and directions on packet. Strain and while still warm place in a bowl and pour over the French dressing. Toss the warm rice in the dressing to coat and add the sultanas, stirring through well. Leave on one side.

Heat the oil in a saucepan and sauté the onion for about 5 minutes, stirring occasionally. Add the apple and cook for another 2-3 minutes. Stir in the flour and curry powder, cook for another couple of minutes and then stir in the chutney and the tomatoes. Cover the saucepan and simmer gently for 30 minutes. Allow sauce to cool.

Mix together the mayonnaise, lemon juice, seasoning and Tabasco and stir this into the cooled sauce. Stir in the prawns and put the bowl to chill in the refrigerator until you are ready to serve.

Place the dressed rice mixture on a serving dish and spoon the prawn mixture over the rice.

To garnish sprinkle with chopped parsley mixed with chopped chives.

~

Rainbow Trout with Almonds and More

SERVES 4

4 rainbow trout, cleaned
2 oz (50 g) flour
salt and freshly ground black
    pepper
1 aubergine
3 large tomatoes
½ cucumber
6 oz (175 g) butter
3 tablespoons oil
1 clove garlic, chopped
8 lemon slices
2 oz (50 g) toasted flaked
    almonds
1 tablespoon chopped parsley

IF AT ALL POSSIBLE I STRONGLY RECOMMEND THAT FOR ANY TROUT RECIPE YOU SEEK OUT FRESHLY CAUGHT WILD FISH. DIFFICULT I KNOW, BUT THE DIFFERENCE IS REMARKABLE. FASHIONABLE FOOD WRITERS TEND TO LOOK DOWN ON THE WELL KNOWN TROUT AND ALMONDS FOUND ON FAR TOO MANY RESTAURANT MENUS BUT THIS DISH COULD WELL PERSUADE THEM TO EAT THEIR WORDS.

Wash and gently pat dry the trout, then dust with the flour, seasoned with salt and pepper.

Slice the aubergine thickly across and then cut into cubes. Slice the tomatoes across in three and then halve the slices. Peel the cucumber and cut the flesh into small cubes.

Melt 2 oz (50 g) of the butter with 2 tablespoons of oil in a pan and gently fry the fish for 4-5 minutes on each side until cooked. Remove and keep warm on a serving dish.

Wipe out the pan and melt 2 oz (50 g) butter with 1 tablespoon oil, add the aubergine cubes and fry for 1 minute then add the tomatoes and cucumber and continue to cook until heated through. Arrange this vegetable mixture around the trout and then quickly melt the remaining 2 oz (50 g) butter in the pan until sizzling. Add the chopped garlic, stir-fry for 15 seconds and spoon the garlic butter over the fish.

Finally surround the dish with lemon slices, toasted almonds and parsley.

~

Remarkable Rice

SERVES 4

*10 oz (275 g) uncooked long
   grain rice*
salt
1 onion
1 clove garlic
1 green pepper
3 tomatoes
2 tablespoons oil
4 oz (110 g) frozen peas
2 oz (50 g) pine kernels
6 oz (175 g) peeled prawns
freshly ground black pepper
3 oz (75 g) Swiss cheese, grated
*1 oz (25 g) Parmesan cheese,
   grated*

SO CALLED 'SPECIALITY' RICE DISHES HAVE RECENTLY EMERGED AS QUITE AN IMPORTANT FEATURE ON THE SUPERMARKET SHELVES AND IN FREEZERS AND CLEARLY THE MARKET IS GROWING FOR FOOD THAT IS SLIGHTLY DIFFERENT. JUST RUN YOUR EYE DOWN THE LIST OF IN-GREDIENTS HERE AND YOU WILL SEE STRAIGHTAWAY THE GREAT VALUE ALL ROUND OF RICE-BASED DIY DISHES.

Cook the rice in a large saucepan of boiling salted water for 12 minutes. Strain and keep warm.

Next chop the onion, and crush the clove of garlic. Remove the core and seeds from the green pepper, and chop finely. Cover the tomatoes with boiling water for about 30 seconds. Strain and then remove their skins. These should slip off easily. Chop the tomato flesh.

Heat the oil in a large frying pan and add the onion, garlic and the green pepper. Cook gently until soft. Then add the chopped tomatoes and the peas. Cook for a few minutes more, add the pine kernels followed by the prawns. Season with black pepper and warm through for another minute, then gently mix the whole contents of the pan with the cooked rice.

Pile the mixture into a well buttered ovenproof dish. Mix the two cheeses together and sprinkle over the top.

Bake in the oven at 400°F-200°C-Gas Mark 6 until brown and bubbly on top.

Serve straightaway with a fresh tomato salad.

~

Skate in Black Butter

SERVES 4

4 skate wings
water
4 tablespoons wine vinegar
5 lemon slices
bouquet garni
3 sprigs parsley, with stalks
6 onion rings
salt and pepper
1 tablespoon chopped parsley
2 teaspoons capers
4 oz (110 g) butter

ONE OF THE TRULY GREAT FISH CREATIONS WHICH I SUSPECT IS HARDLY EVER ATTEMPTED IN THE HOME KITCHEN. PLEASE GIVE IT A TRY.

Take a wide flat pan and put in about ¼ pint (150 ml) water, 2 tablespoons of wine vinegar, lemon slices, bouquet garni, parsley sprigs and onion rings, salt and pepper.

Put the fish into the mixture, adding a little water if necessary to cover the fish. Bring to the boil, turn down the heat and simmer for 10-15 minutes. Drain the fish and place on a warmed serving dish and sprinkle with the chopped parsley.

In a bowl mix together the capers and the other 2 tablespoons of wine vinegar. Keep to one side.

Place a frying pan over a high heat. Put the 4 oz (110 g) butter into the very hot pan, the butter will foam and turn a dark golden brown. Pour the hot, foaming butter over the fish. Then quickly in the same pan, pour in the caper and wine vinegar mixture. Bring to a fast boil and pour over the fish.

Serve immediately with plain boiled or mashed potatoes.

～

Sole with Curry Cream

SERVES 4

*8 fillets Dover or lemon sole (or
    brill or other fresh white fish)*
salt and pepper
juice of ½ lemon
glass dry white wine
½ glass water

for the sauce
2 oz (50 g) butter
1 onion, finely chopped
*½ teaspoon mild curry powder
    or paste*
*½ teaspoon ginger root, finely
    chopped*
1 tablespoon plain flour
8 oz (225 g) cooked prawns
¼ pint (150 ml) double cream
1 tablespoon chopped parsley

THIS CLEARLY BELONGS TO THE SPECIAL OCCASION CATEGORY. FOR PREFERENCE I WOULD CHOOSE EITHER DOVER SOLE OR BRILL FILLETS BECAUSE APART FROM THEIR SUPERIOR FLAVOUR THERE IS LESS CHANCE OF THE FILLETS BREAKING UP WHEN YOU SERVE THEM.

Lay the fillets in a buttered ovenproof dish, season them with salt and pepper and the juice of ½ lemon. Pour over a glass of dry white wine and ½ glass water. Cover with foil or buttered paper and bake in the oven at 350°F-180°C-Gas Mark 4 for about 15 minutes.

When cooked pour off the cooking liquor and reserve, and cover the fish and keep warm.

Before the fish completes its cooking begin to make the sauce. Melt the butter and soften the onion with the ½ teaspoon curry powder or paste and the chopped ginger root. Cook gently for about 10 minutes. Stir in the flour and cook for just 1 minute, stirring gently, then add the prawns and the reserved cooking liquor from the fish. Allow to cook very gently for about 5-6 minutes adding some more white wine if you prefer a thinner sauce.

Just before serving stir in ¼ pint (150 ml) of double cream and a tablespoon of chopped parsley. Heat to just below boiling point and pour over the fish fillets. Boiled rice makes an excellent accompaniment to this lovely dish.

~

Tuna Treat

2 × 7 oz (2 × 100 g) cans tuna
  fish
2 tablespoons soy sauce
2 tablespoons sherry
¼ teaspoon ground ginger
pepper to taste
1 bunch of spring onions
1 red pepper
7 oz (200 g) mange tout
1 small tin water chestnuts
2 fl oz (55 ml) oil
2 oz (50 g) cashew nuts

IN THE CHINESE STIR-FRY STYLE THIS COLOURFUL MIXTURE, IN LOOKS ALONE, CAN DO A LOT FOR JADED PALATES.

Break the tuna fish into chunks and place in a bowl. Add the soy sauce, sherry, ginger and some pepper to the fish.

Slice the spring onions, including the green part, into 1" (2.5 cm) pieces. Core and de-seed the red pepper and cut into strips. Top and tail the mange tout. Drain and slice the water chestnuts.

Heat the oil in a wok or pan and stir-fry the spring onions, red pepper and mange tout for 2-3 minutes. Add the tuna fish mixture with the water chestnuts and continue to cook for 2-3 minutes until warmed through.

Serve this with rice and scatter the cashew nuts over the top just before serving.

~

Vinegar Fish

SERVES 4

2 lb (900 g) white fish fillets
2 tablespoons flour
salt and pepper
2 oz (50 g) butter
2 large onions, thinly sliced
4 fl oz (110 ml) white wine
  vinegar
2 teaspoons dry mustard
  powder
2 cloves garlic, crushed
1 teaspoon oregano, chopped
2 tablespoons parsley, chopped
½ teaspoon fresh coriander,
  chopped
1 tablespoon lemon juice
small glass of white wine or dry
  cider
4 fl oz (110 ml) oil

FULL OF TASTE, THIS RATHER UNUSUAL COMBINATION OF FLAVOURS WILL APPEAL TO THOSE WHO LIKE TO EXPERIMENT.

Pat the fish fillets dry with kitchen paper. Season the flour with salt and pepper and dust the fish fillets with the flour, and then arrange them in a lightly buttered shallow ovenproof dish.

Heat the butter in a pan and gently fry the onions until soft, then spread the onions over the top of the fish fillets.

In a bowl blend together the vinegar, mustard powder, garlic, oregano, parsley, coriander, lemon juice, wine and lastly the oil.

When well blended together pour this dressing over the fish and bake in the oven at 350°F-180°C-Gas Mark 4 for about 45 minutes.

~

By far the best way of ensuring a satis-factory supply of good tasty meat is to have a personal independent butcher with whom you can build a mutually re-warding relationship. However I realise that for the majority of people today this isn't possible, especially with modern shopping trends and working commit-ments.

Some supermarkets however do have a butcher behind the scenes who will be more than pleased to see you if you have a particular requirement.

Look out too for the 'traditional' organically grown meat (Sainsbury's have it for example) which has been pro-perly aged before sale. They charge more for it because it is more expensive to pro-duce, but, if you can afford it, it's well worth the extra cost.

Beaujolais Beef

SERVES 4

1½ lb (700 g) top rump
1 tablespoon flour
salt and pepper
2 tablespoons oil
2 oz (50 g) butter
2 onions, sliced
1 clove garlic, crushed
1 tablespoon tomato purée
8 oz (225 g) pitted prunes
½ teaspoon cinnamon
½ teaspoon mixed spice
½ pint (275 ml) Beaujolais or
   other red wine
½ pint (275 ml) beef stock

I FIRST MADE THIS DISH IN THE MONTH OF NOVEMBER TO COINCIDE WITH THE ANNUAL ARRIVAL OF THE 'BEAUJOLAIS NOUVEAU'. ALTHOUGH ANY REASONABLE RED WINE CAN BE USED, THE 'BETTER THE WINE THE BETTER THE SAUCE' RULE APPLIES, AS WITH ANY OTHER DISH.

Preheat the oven to 350°F-180°C-Gas Mark 4.

Cut the meat into cubes. Season the flour with salt and pepper and dust the meat in the seasoned flour.

Heat the oil and fry the meat cubes until browned on all sides. Lift out and transfer to a casserole dish.

In a clean pan melt the butter and fry the onions with the garlic until soft. Add the tomato purée and when well mixed, stir into the casserole, and mix well with the meat. Next, scatter the prunes, cinnamon and spice over the meat and onions, and pour in the Beaujolais and stock. Cover and cook in the oven for 1½ hours. Check occasionally and if needed top up the liquid with additional stock or wine.

When the meat is tender, serve with boiled rice.

~

Beef Stroganoff

SERVES 4

1 lb (450 g) fillet of beef
1 medium onion
1 tablespoon oil
1 oz (25 g) butter
1 teaspoon dry English mustard
   powder
1 tablespoon paprika
salt
1 tablespoon tomato purée
¼ pint (150 ml) beef stock
5 fl oz (150 ml) soured cream

COUNT PAUL STROGANOFF WAS A NINETEENTH-CENTURY RUSSIAN GOURMET WHOSE CHEF INVENTED THIS NOW WORLD-FAMOUS CLASSIC, WHICH IS STILL VERY POPULAR ON RESTAURANT MENUS BECAUSE IT'S QUITE EASY AND QUICK TO PREPARE. THIS ALSO MAKES IT IDEAL FOR HOME ENTERTAINING. SERVE WITH PLAIN BOILED RICE OR NOODLES TO SOAK UP THE RICH VELVETY SAUCE.

Slice the beef fillet into very thin slices, and chop the onion.

Melt the oil and butter in a saucepan and add the onions and the beef. Cook, stirring gently until the onions are soft and the meat coloured. Then add to the pan the mustard powder and paprika. Stir in well and add salt. Next mix in the tomato purée and when it is well blended with the other ingredients, add the stock.

Allow to simmer for 15 minutes.

Then remove from the heat and stir in the soured cream.

Warm gently – DO NOT ALLOW TO BOIL – and serve immediately.

Boeuf Bourguignon

SERVES 4

2 lb (900 g) braising steak or
  top rump
4 oz (110 g) piece of bacon, de-
  rinded
2 tablespoons oil
2 oz (50 g) butter
2 cloves garlic, crushed
2 tablespoons plain flour
salt and freshly ground black
  pepper
bouquet garni
½ pint (275 ml) red wine,
  Burgundy, if possible
¼ pint (150 ml) beef stock
12 whole small onions, skinned
1 dessertspoon sugar
12 button mushrooms
chopped parsley to garnish

optional additional
  vegetables
2 carrots
1 leek
4 shallots
1 onion

I'M SURE THIS RECIPE NEEDS NO INTRODUCTION, AND MADE AS
DIRECTED HERE IT IS STILL A GREAT DISH AND IN THESE POST-
NOUVELLE CUISINE DAYS, WELL WORTH REVIVING.

Trim the steak and cut into cubes. Dice the bacon.

In a large flameproof casserole heat 1 tablespoon oil with 1 oz
(25 g) butter and quickly brown the diced bacon. Remove with a
slotted spoon. The brown the meat on all sides. Return the bacon
to the casserole with the crushed garlic. Sprinkle the flour over
and stir in well. Add salt and pepper, the bouquet garni, the wine
and enough stock to cover the meat. Bring to the boil, stirring
gently all the time. Cover and cook in the oven at 325°F-170°C-Gas
Mark 3 for 1½ hours.

Meanwhile heat the remaining oil and butter together and
sauté the whole onions with the sugar until they become glazed
all over. Remove from the pan and then sauté the mushrooms.
After the casserole has cooked for the 1½ hours add the onions
and mushrooms and return to the oven for a further 30 minutes.
When the cooking time is up remove the bouquet garni and skim
off any surplus fat.

Garnish with chopped parsley.

Note: If you prefer to add the additional vegetables then simply
chop them all and add to the casserole just before you pour in the
wine and stock.

~

Chilli Cassoulet

SERVES 4

1 lb (450 g) chuck steak
4 oz (110 g) onion
2 tablespoons oil
15 oz (425 g) can red kidney
  beans, drained
8 oz (225 g) can cannellini
  beans, drained
1 teaspoon chilli powder
salt and freshly ground black
  pepper
½ pint (275 ml) beef stock

A LITTLE CROSS-POLLINATION HERE BETWEEN THE FRENCH BEAN
CASSOULET AND MEXICAN CHILLI – AND IT WORKS!

Trim the steak and slice the onion.

In a pan heat the oil and fry the beef and onion together for
about 5 minutes. Place them in an ovenproof casserole dish with
the kidney and cannellini beans, chilli powder and seasonings.
Pour over the stock, cover and cook in the oven at 325°F-170°C-
Gas Mark 3 for 2½ hours.

Serve with baked jacket potatoes.

Cornish Pot Roast

SERVES 4

*4 × 6 oz (175 g) rump steak
  slices
plain flour
salt and pepper
1 oz (25 g) butter
2 tbs oil
1 large bay leaf, crushed
2 large onions, sliced
4 potatoes, peeled and thinly
  sliced
beef stock
chopped parsley to garnish*

THIS TRADITIONAL CORNISH-STYLE POT ROAST HAS NEVER FAILED TO PLEASE. THE INGREDIENTS ARE SIMPLE AND ALWAYS AVAILABLE. I AS FAR AS THE STOCK IS CONCERNED ALWAYS USE EITHER THE FRESH REAL BEEF STOCK SOLD IN MOST SUPERMARKETS IN HALF PINT TUBS OR TINNED BEEF CONSOMMÉ.

Use a rolling pin dipped in water to sharply bash each piece of meat three or four times, which will break down the sinews.

Roll up the steak slices into fat 'cigars' and dust all over with the flour which you have seasoned well with salt and pepper.

Melt the butter and oil in a large frying pan and when the butter starts to foam briskly brown the steak rolls and then transfer to an ovenproof casserole or pot, in one layer. Scatter the crushed bay leaf on top and then cover with the sliced onions followed by another sprinkling of salt and pepper and then the potato slices. Season lightly again and carefully pour over sufficient stock to come about half way up the potato layer.

If wished, a few flecks of butter can be dotted over the potatoes.

Bake in the oven without any cover at 400°F 200°C Gas Mark 6 for about 50 to 60 minutes until the potatoes are fully cooked through. (Test with a sharp pronged fork.)

Serve with a generous garnish of finely chopped parsley and any seasonal vegetable.

~

Devilled Steak

SERVES 2

2 × 6 oz (175 g) sirloin steaks
oil
6 tablespoons yoghurt (Greek if
    possible)
2 teaspoons made mustard
    (mild or hot)
2 teaspoons Worcestershire
    sauce
salt and freshly ground black
    pepper
chopped chives or parsley to
    garnish

IF YOU'RE LOOKING FOR A LOW-FAT ALTERNATIVE TO DOUBLE CREAM, THEN YOGHURT FITS THE BILL. THE TYPE OF MUSTARD THAT CAN BE USED IS DOWN TO PERSONAL CHOICE SINCE HEATING MUSTARD OF ANY STRENGTH WILL REDUCE ITS 'BITE'.

Brush the steaks with a little oil and then fry until cooked to either rare, medium or well-done, as preferred.

Meanwhile make a sauce by combining the yoghurt, mustard, Worcestershire sauce and salt and pepper in a bowl, and mix well together.

When the steaks are cooked pour the yoghurt mixture over them in the pan, and move the meat around gently as you heat the sauce through.

Lift the steaks on to a serving dish, pour over the sauce and sprinkle with chopped chives or parsley.

~

Greek Macaroni Bake

SERVES 4

2 tablespoons oil
2 onions, finely chopped
1 lb (450 g) beef or lamb,
    minced
3 tablespoons tomato purée
salt
1 clove garlic, crushed
½ teaspoon marjoram, chopped
8 oz (225 g) long macaroni or
    rigatoni
1 oz (25 g) Cheddar cheese,
    grated

for the sauce
1 oz (25 g) butter
1 oz (25 g) flour
1 pint (570 ml) warm milk
¼ teaspoon freshly grated
    nutmeg
black pepper

I THINK OF THIS AS A VERY FRIENDLY DISH. THERE IS NOTHING REALLY COMPLICATED HERE, JUST PLENTY OF STRAIGHTFORWARD FLAVOUR FOR ALL-ROUND POPULARITY.

Heat the oil in a frying pan. Add the onions and fry until lightly browned. Add the minced meat, and cook stirring until browned. Then add the tomato purée, a little salt, garlic and marjoram. Cook, stirring frequently, for about 10 minutes. Remove from the heat.

Meanwhile cook the macaroni in plenty of boiling salted water for 10 minutes until just tender. Drain. Lay the macaroni in the base of a large greased ovenproof dish.

For the sauce, melt the butter in a pan and add the flour, cook stirring for 1 minute. Gradually add the warm milk, nutmeg and salt and pepper to taste.

Spoon a third of the sauce over the macaroni.

Spread the meat mixture carefully over the top and then cover with the remaining sauce.

Sprinkle the grated cheese over the top and bake in the oven at 375°F-190°C-Gas Mark 5 for 40-45 minutes until golden brown.

SERVES 4

2 lb (900 g) stewing beef
seasoned flour
3 tablespoons oil
2 large onions, chopped
2 teaspoons sugar
1 teaspoon dry English mustard
1 tablespoon tomato purée
1 thick strip of orange peel
1 bay leaf
1 teaspoon thyme, chopped
1 pint (570 ml) Guinness
salt and pepper

for the dumplings
4 oz (110 g) self-raising flour
pinch of salt
2 oz (50 g) shredded suet
cold water to mix
2-3 tablespoons chopped parsley

Guinnessed Beef with Parsley Dumplings

THIS DISH IS A REAL WINTER-WARMER, FAMILY-FILLER AND GOOD ENOUGH FOR GUESTS. NOTHING MORE NEEDS TO BE SAID.

Trim the meat and cut into cubes. Toss in the seasoned flour.

Heat 2 tablespoons of oil in a pan and brown the cubes of meat on all sides. Remove from the pan.

Add the remaining oil to the pan and fry the onions until soft. Add the sugar, mustard powder, tomato purée, orange peel, bay leaf and thyme to the pan and mix well. Pour in the Guinness and bring to the boil, stirring everything together. Season with a little salt and pepper.

Return the meat to the pan, cover and simmer for 2-2½ hours, or until the meat is tender. Alternatively you can cook in a casserole in the oven at 300°F-150°C-Gas Mark 2.

About 30 minutes before the end of the cooking time prepare and cook the dumplings. In a bowl mix the flour, salt and suet together. Add enough cold water to make a pliable dough.

Turn out the dough on to a floured board, sprinkle with the chopped parsley and knead lightly, working the parsley into the mixture. Divide the mixture into 8 balls and cook in a saucepan of simmering beef stock or water for about 20 minutes.

Lift out with a slotted spoon and serve with the beef.

~

Russian Casserole (page 57) and
Guinnessed Beef with Parsley Dumplings.

Hungarian Goulash

2 lb (900 g) braising steak
4 tablespoons oil
2 onions, thinly sliced
1 clove garlic, crushed
3 tablespoons plain flour
2 tablespoons paprika
salt and pepper
2 × 14 oz (396 g) cans tomatoes
1 tablespoon tomato purée
2 bay leaves
2 teaspoons sugar
1 red pepper, de-seeded and
   chopped
5 fl oz (150 ml) soured cream
8 toast triangles
chopped parsley to garnish

HUNGARY'S WORLD-FAMOUS BEEF STEW, WELL FLAVOURED WITH
THAT COUNTRY'S BELOVED PAPRIKA. ORIGINALLY A PEASANT DISH,
THIS VERSION INCLUDES THE TRANSYLVANIAN ADDITION OF SOURED
CREAM, STIRRED THROUGH AT THE LAST MOMENT, WHICH IMPROVES
BOTH APPEARANCE AND TASTE.

Trim the braising steak, removing any fat, and cut the meat into
strips.

Heat 2 tablespoons of oil in a frying pan and cook the onion and
garlic until soft. Remove from the heat and reserve.

In a bowl mix together the flour, paprika and salt and pepper.
Coat the meat strips in this seasoned flour mixture.

Heat the remaining 2 tablespoons of oil in a flameproof casserole and add the meat and fry over a high heat until browned on
all sides. Stir in any remaining flour and the tomatoes, tomato
purée, bay leaves, sugar and the fried onions.

Bring to the boil, cover and simmer for 1½ hours. Then add the
chopped red pepper and continue to simmer for a further 30
minutes. Stir in the soured cream, surround with toast triangles
and sprinkle with chopped parsley before serving.

~

Extra Irish Stew (page 80) and
Rich Beef Pie (page 56).

Lancashire Beef Pie

SERVES 4

for the pastry
12 oz (350 g) plain flour
pinch of salt
3 oz (75 g) lard
3 oz (75 g) margarine
cold water to mix

for the filling
1 tablespoon oil
1 large onion, chopped
1 stick celery, chopped
1 lb (450 g) minced beef
salt and black pepper
1 tablespoon Worcestershire
  sauce
10 slices of black pudding
1 egg beaten

A DISTINCTIVE FEATURE OF THIS DISH IS THE SLICED BLACK PUDDING, WHICH ENJOYS GREATER POPULARITY IN THE NORTH OF ENGLAND THAN IN THE SOUTH. TRADITIONALLY MADE WITH PIG'S BLOOD, OAT-MEAL, PORK FAT, ONION AND HERBS, THE LARGE BLACK SAUSAGE RINGS ARE PRE-COOKED BY BOILING. THEY ARE ALSO DELICIOUS SLICED AND FRIED OR GRILLED, ESPECIALLY ACCOMPANIED BY BOTTLED BROWN SAUCE. WELL WORTH TRYING, AND IF YOU HAVEN'T ALREADY, THIS RECIPE MAKES A VERY TASTY INTRODUCTION.

Preheat the oven to 350°F-180°C-Gas Mark 4.

Make the pastry by sifting the flour and salt into a bowl. Add the fats cut into cubes and rub in until the mixture resembles breadcrumbs. Using a knife mix in a little water to form a stiff dough. Allow to chill for 20 minutes before rolling out.

For the filling, heat the oil in a pan and gently soften the onion and celery for about 5 minutes. Then add the minced beef, salt and pepper with the Worcestershire sauce. Cook, stirring, until browned.

Cut one third off the pastry and reserve. Roll out the other two-thirds to line a greased 8" (20 cm) pie dish.

Pile the beef and onion mixture into the pastry case and arrange the black pudding slices over the top. Roll out the remaining pastry and moisten the edges before placing over the pie. Press the edges together and knock up. Make a couple of slits in the top of the pastry, decorate if wished, and brush with beaten egg.

Bake in the oven for 30 minutes.

~

Lentil Flan

SERVES 4

6 oz (175 g) lentils
1 onion, finely chopped
1 pint (570 ml) milk
salt and black pepper
½ teaspoon ground nutmeg
1 lb (450 g) minced beef
2 oz (50 g) fresh breadcrumbs
1 teaspoon tomato purée
2 cloves garlic, crushed
2 teaspoons French mustard
2 eggs, whisked, in two bowls
3 oz (75 g) Cheddar cheese

SOME PEOPLE LAUGH AT LENTILS AND I REALLY CAN'T FIGURE OUT WHY. THEY ARE AN EXCELLENT SOURCE OF PROTEIN AND VERY PLEASANT TO EAT. THE 'FLAN' HERE IS QUITE NOVEL BEING MADE OF LIGHTLY SPICED MINCED BEEF.

Put the lentils and onion into a saucepan with the milk. Bring to the boil, cover and simmer gently, stirring occasionally, for about 1 hour, until you have a thick mixture. Season with salt, pepper and nutmeg.

Put the minced beef into a bowl with plenty of salt and pepper. Add the breadcrumbs, tomato purée, garlic, mustard and 1 whisked egg. Mix everything well together.

Preheat the oven to 350°F-180°C-Gas Mark 4.

Grease a 9" (23 cm) flan dish. Line the dish with the meat mixture, pressing it over the bottom, and up the sides.

Add the remaining egg to the lentil mixture, stir well and spoon into the meat casing.

Sprinkle the grated cheese over the top and cook in the centre of the oven for 45-50 minutes until the filling has set.

~

Ossobucco

2½ lb (1.25 kg) shin of veal
2 oz (50 g) butter
2 onions, finely chopped
2 carrots, finely chopped
2 sticks celery, finely chopped
1 clove garlic, finely chopped
2 strips of lemon peel
plain flour for dusting
salt and pepper
8 tablespoons vegetable oil
½ pint (275 ml) dry white wine
½ pint (275 ml) chicken stock
14 oz (396 g) can tomatoes,
    roughly chopped
1 teaspoon thyme, chopped
2 bay leaves
3 sprigs parsley

for the gremolada
1 teaspoon lemon zest
1 tablespoon chopped parsley
1 clove garlic, chopped

JUST ONE OF THE MANY GREAT DISHES FROM ITALY. A WORD IN ADVANCE WITH YOUR BUTCHER IS NECESSARY AND DON'T NEGLECT TO TIE THE SHIN PIECES TOGETHER OTHERWISE THEY WILL FALL MELTINGLY FROM THE BONE. THE GREMOLADA TOPS THE LOT AS A GARNISH.

Preheat the oven to 350°F-180°C-Gas Mark 4.

Cut the shin of veal into pieces about 2″ (5 cm) long and tie each one around the middle with string.

Use a large flameproof casserole with a lid that can take the veal pieces in a single layer or a roasting tin with doubled foil for a lid.

Melt the butter and cook the onion, carrot and celery for 10 minutes until soft. Then add the garlic and strips of lemon peel. Remove from the heat.

Dust the veal pieces in seasoned flour. In a large frying pan heat the oil and brown the veal on both sides and then place on top of the vegetables in the casserole. Spoon out most of the fat from the frying pan and then pour in the wine and allow to bubble for 2-3 minutes. Pour over the veal in the casserole.

Heat the chicken stock and add to the casserole, followed by the tomatoes, thyme, bay leaves, parsley and salt and pepper to taste. The meat should now be covered, if not add more stock.

Simmer and cover tightly and place in the lower third of the oven for about 2 hours. The sauce should be fairly thick; if not, place the veal on a warm dish and bring the sauce to the boil in the casserole until it thickens and then pour over the veal and serve.

A traditional garnish is gremolada. Simply combine the lemon zest, parsley and garlic together and sprinkle over the top of the finished dish just before serving.

~

Perfect Pot Roast

SERVES 6

2 oz (50 g) beef dripping

3 lb (1⅓ kg) boned rolled brisket
 of beef

4 small whole onions, or 2
 medium onions, peeled and
 quartered

2 cloves garlic, chopped
 (optional)

4 ribs of celery, cut into thirds

4 carrots, peeled and cut into
 thirds

15 oz (425 g) can chopped
 tomatoes

4 oz (110 g) button mushrooms

1 teaspoon oregano

1 sprig thyme

1 bay leaf

salt and pepper

½ pint (275 fl oz) beef stock or

¼ pint (150 fl oz) stock and ¼
 pint (150 fl oz) red wine

1 tablespoon flour

1 tablespoon butter

chopped parsley to garnish

THIS IS ONE OF THE TRULY GREAT ENGLISH DISHES. HERE IT IS EN-
HANCED BY THE ADDITION OF SOME WONDERFUL EUROPEAN INGRE-
DIENTS – TOMATOES, GARLIC, OREGANO AND RED WINE STOCK.

Preheat the oven to 275°F-140°C-Gas Mark 1.

Melt the dripping in a heavy pot and when hot, brown the meat
all over.

Remove the meat to a plate, then into the pot put the onions,
garlic, celery and carrots, and fry together, gently, for a few
minutes. Next, add the tomatoes and mushrooms, and when
they are hot, return the meat to the pot. Now add the oregano,
thyme, bay leaf, a little salt and pepper and the hot stock.

Cover with a tight fitting lid (use foil if necessary to improve the
seal) and as soon as you hear the contents start to simmer, place in
the centre of the oven, and leave to cook for 3 hours. When
cooked, arrange the meat on a serving platter with the vegetables.

Blend together the flour and butter. On the top of the stove boil
the remaining liquid and thicken by whisking in the flour and butter paste. Pour around the meat and vegetables and sprinkle on
some chopped parsley.

Serve the meat sliced, with boiled potatoes and English
mustard.

～

Rich Beef Pie

SERVES 4

1¼ lb (570 g) chuck steak
¼ lb (110 g) kidney
1 tablespoon finely chopped
*   onion*
2 teaspoons marjoram, chopped
salt and freshly ground black
*   pepper*
¼ pint (150 ml) dry red wine
little dripping
1 level tablespoon flour
8 oz (225 g) puff pastry
beaten egg to glaze

THIS IS OF COURSE A KIND OF STEAK AND KIDNEY PIE ENRICHED BY OVERNIGHT MARINADING IN A LITTLE RED WINE WITH ONION AND MARJORAM. BEEF KIDNEY WOULD BE CORRECT TO USE BUT IF YOU FIND THIS A LITTLE TOO STRONG THEN I SUGGEST YOU USE LAMB'S KIDNEY.

Trim the beef and cut both the steak and kidney into pieces. Place them in a bowl and cover with the onion, marjoram, seasoning and the wine. Turn the meat in the marinade, cover and leave overnight in the refrigerator.

When ready to cook, drain the meat and reserve the marinade. Melt a little dripping in a pan and when hot fry the meat to seal. Sprinkle the flour over the meat, stir well and gradually add the marinade to the pan. Taste for seasoning.

Turn into a 1½ pint (850 ml) pie dish, and allow to cool before covering with the pastry lid. Roll out the pastry slightly larger than the dish and cut off a strip from around the pastry edges. Moisten and press on to the rim of the pie dish. Moisten again and press on the remaining pastry for the lid. Knock up the edges and then brush with beaten egg. Mark slits across the top with a knife, and decorate with pastry leaves, if wished.

Bake in the centre of the oven at 450°F-230°C-Gas Mark 8 for 15 minutes. Then reduce the oven temperature to 350°F-180°C-Gas Mark 4 for a further 2 hours or until the meat is tender.

After ¾ hour of baking cover the pastry with foil to prevent over browning.

~

Russian Casserole

1½ lb (700 g) stewing beef
1 tablespoon plain flour
salt and pepper
1 teaspoon curry powder
1 tablespoon oil
2 large onions, sliced
8 oz (225 g) parsnip, peeled and
   sliced
½ pint (275 ml) beef stock
2 tablespoons tomato purée
¼ pint (150 ml) soured cream
1½ lb (700 g) potatoes, peeled,
   sliced, ¼" (5 mm) thick

THIS IS A GREAT DISH FULL OF SATISFYING FLAVOUR CREATED BY THE INTERESTING COMBINATION OF CURRY SPICES, PARSNIPS AND SOURED CREAM. IDEAL FOR UNCOMPLICATED HOME ENTERTAINING.

Preheat the oven to 325°F-170°C-Gas Mark 3.

Trim the meat and cut into cubes. Mix together the flour, salt, pepper and curry powder and toss the cubes of meat in this mixture.

Heat the oil in a frying pan and brown the meat on all sides. Transfer to a casserole dish.

Fry the onions in the remaining oil and add to the meat, along with the sliced parsnip.

Put the remaining seasoned flour into the pan along with the stock and tomato pureé and stir well. Bring just to boiling point. Immediately stir in the soured cream and pour over the contents of the casserole.

Top with overlapping potato slices.

Cover and cook in the oven for 2 hours, then remove the lid from the casserole, increase the oven temperature to 400°F-200°C-Gas Mark 6 and cook for a further 30 minutes to brown the potatoes.

~

Sesame Seed Beef

SERVES 4

2 lb (900 g) sirloin of beef
2 tablespoons oil
6 tablespoons soy sauce
4 tablespoons soft brown sugar
1 tablespoon chilli sauce
1 teaspoon tomato purée
1 tablespoon sesame seeds
1 tablespoon flour
1 medium onion, thinly sliced
1 clove garlic, crushed
6 oz (175 g) button mushrooms
¼ pint (150 ml) water
salt

A VERY GOOD DISH FOR THOSE WITH A PALATE FOR ADVENTURE AND THE FEW HOURS NECESSARY FOR MARINADING. FULL OF DEEP, DARK INTEREST.

Trim the beef and cut into thin strips.

In a large bowl beat together the oil, soy sauce, sugar, chilli sauce and tomato purée. When everything is very well blended work in the sesame seeds and the flour. Then add the beef strips to the bowl with the onion slices and the garlic. Stir through and season with salt.

Cover the bowl and leave to marinade overnight, if possible, or for at least 4 hours in a cool place.

When you are ready to cook, trim the mushrooms, slice them and add to the marinade. Place everything in a large saucepan with ¼ pint (150 ml) of water and bring to the boil, giving a good stir occasionally. Allow to simmer for 15-20 minutes.

Taste and, if necessary, adjust seasoning. Serve with rice.

~

Special Moussaka

1 large aubergine, thinly sliced
3 tablespoons oil
1 medium onion, finely chopped
1 lb (450 g) minced beef
1 tablespoon paprika
1 clove garlic, crushed
2 tablespoons tomato purée
4 oz (110 g) mushrooms,
   chopped
½ pint (275 ml) beef stock
salt and pepper

for the topping
¼ pint (150 ml) plain yoghurt
1 egg
3 oz (75 g) Cheddar cheese,
   grated

PERSONALLY I HAVE NEVER BOTHERED WITH PRE-SALTING CERTAIN VEGETABLES TO REMOVE MOISTURE. I HAVE BEEN TOLD THAT TODAY'S VARIETIES, INCLUDING AUBERGINE, DON'T NEED THIS TREATMENT, SO PLEASE FEEL FREE TO FOLLOW ME IF YOU WISH. THIS RECIPE, BY THE WAY, GIVES A SMASHING RESULT AND MAY LARGELY BE ASSEMBLED THE DAY BEFORE EATING.

Preheat the oven to 375°F-190°C-Gas Mark 5.

Arrange the aubergine slices on lightly oiled baking sheets and bake in a preheated oven for 15 minutes.

Meanwhile make the meat sauce. Fry the onion in the remaining oil for two minutes. Add the minced beef and cook, stirring, until lightly browned. Stir in the paprika and cook for one minute. Add the garlic, tomato purée, mushrooms, stock and salt and pepper. Cover and simmer the sauce for 15 minutes.

In a greased ovenproof dish arrange the meat sauce and aubergine slices in alternate layers, starting with meat sauce and ending with a layer of aubergine. Brush the top with oil and cover the dish with foil.

Bake in the oven for 20 minutes.*

Beat the yoghurt with the egg and grated cheese and spoon the mixture over the top of the moussaka and bake for a further 15 minutes.

* If eating the following day, remove from the oven after the first 20 minutes, allow to cool and place in the refrigerator overnight. On the day of eating, proceed with the yoghurt mixture and bake in the preheated oven for about 25 minutes.

～

Steak and Kidney Pudding

SERVES 4

8 oz (225 g) suet pastry
1 lb (450 g) stewing steak,
trimmed
4 oz (110 g) ox kidney
flour
salt and pepper
beef stock or water

I'VE INCLUDED THIS GREAT OLD FAVOURITE, WHICH DOES TAKE TIME TO PREPARE, BECAUSE PEOPLE LOVE IT – AND THAT'S A GOOD ENOUGH REASON TO GIVE IT A SHOWING ONE WET AND DREARY WINTER WEEK-END.

First line a greased 2 pint (1 litre) pudding basin with the pastry. The best way to do this is to take a piece of string and holding one end at the top of the basin, run the string down the side, across the base and up the far side of the basin. Where the string reaches the far rim, cut the string.

Roll out the pastry to a round, making the diameter of the round the same as the length of the string. Cut out a quarter wedge.

Lift the larger piece of pastry into the greased basin. Join the edges and press well on to the base and sides.

Next, trim and cut the steak and kidney into cubes, and toss all the meat in the flour, seasoned with salt and pepper. Place the meat in the lined basin, and pour in enough stock or water to come two-thirds of the way up the basin.

Roll out the remaining quarter of the pastry into a round to fit the top of the basin. Dampen the edges and put on the pastry lid. Press the edges to seal.

Cover the pudding with greaseproof paper and foil and secure under the rim with string.

Allow to steam for 4 hours.

~

Chicken (and turkey too) has excellent nutritional value, being very high in protein content and lower in calories than most other meats. It's also wonderfully adaptable to all methods of seasoning and cooking, which must account for its deserved popularity. The following selection of recipes demonstrates its versatility to delicious effect.

Atlantic Chicken

SERVES 4

4 chicken portions
salt and pepper
2 tablespoons oil
2 large ribs celery, sliced
1 large onion, sliced
1 small green pepper, de-seeded
*   and cut in strips*
1½-2 oz (40g-50g) preserved
*   ginger, chopped*
1 tablespoon ginger syrup
10 fl oz (275 ml) chicken stock
1½ level teaspoons cornflour
cold water

THIS IS REALLY A VERY SIMPLE CHICKEN DISH, BUT BY ADDING THE GINGER AND ITS SYRUP YOU CAN MAKE IT RATHER SPECIAL.

Preheat the oven to 350°F-180°C-Gas Mark 4.

Season the chicken pieces with salt and pepper, and then fry them in the oil until lightly browned on both sides. Place them in a shallow flameproof casserole dish.

Fry the celery and onion together until soft. Drain off any remaining fat and then add the green pepper strips to the pan and fry for 2-3 minutes. Add the ginger, the syrup, stock and seasonings and bring to the boil. Pour this over the chicken, cover, and cook in the oven for 50-60 minutes, until tender.

Remove the casserole from the oven.

Blend the cornflour with a little cold water and stir into the casserole. Bring back to the boil on the hob, and simmer for 3 minutes. Adjust the seasoning and serve.

~

Baked Chicken with Mustard and Herbs

SERVES 4

8 chicken pieces, skinned
salt and pepper
2 oz (50 g) plain flour
1 tablespoon Dijon mustard
2 tablespoons made English
*   mustard*
2 egg yolks
2 tablespoons thick cream
2 teaspoons mixed dried herbs
5-6 oz (150-175g) fresh
*   breadcrumbs*

AS THE LIST OF INGREDIENTS SUGGESTS THIS IS A LOVELY RECIPE. ALTHOUGH DRIED MIXED HERBS ARE FINE, FRESH CHIVES, TARRAGON, MARJORAM AND PARSLEY, IF YOU CAN GET SOME, WOULD BE EVEN BETTER — REMEMBER TO DOUBLE AT LEAST THE AMOUNT QUOTED.

Season each chicken piece with salt and pepper and dust with flour.

Mix together the two mustards, the egg yolks and the cream.

In another dish add the herbs to the fresh breadcrumbs.

Dip the chicken pieces first into the mustard mixture, to coat evenly, and then roll in the breadcrumbs and herb mixture, pressing it on firmly.

Chill for 1-2 hours in the fridge to set the coating.

Place the chicken pieces in a well-buttered baking dish and bake in the oven, 375°F-190°C-Gas Mark 5 for about 25 minutes (for boneless pieces) or 40 minutes (on the bone).

Cheesy Chicken

3½ lb (1.5 kg) chicken, cut into
*   pieces*
juice of 1 lemon
salt and freshly ground black
*   pepper*
5 fl oz (150 ml) plain yoghurt
3 tablespoons mayonnaise
1 tablespoon Dijon mustard
dash of Worcestershire sauce
1 teaspoon fresh thyme, chopped
zest of 1 lemon
¼ teaspoon cayenne pepper
3 spring onions, chopped with
*   some green part*
2 oz (50 g) Parmesan cheese,
*   grated*

PEOPLE LOVE THIS DISH; UNDER ITS PALE GOLD PARMESAN CRUST THE OTHER INGREDIENTS BLEND DELICIOUSLY.

Arrange the chicken pieces, skin side up, in a greased ovenproof baking dish. Sprinkle with lemon juice, salt and black pepper.

In a small bowl mix together the yoghurt, mayonnaise, Dijon mustard, Worcestershire sauce, thyme, lemon zest, cayenne pepper and chopped spring onions.

Spread this mixture evenly over the chicken pieces and bake in the oven, uncovered, at 350°F-180°C-Gas Mark 4 for 50 minutes, until the meat is fully cooked.

Remove from the oven and spoon away any excess meat juices.

Sprinkle the chicken with the grated Parmesan cheese and pop under the grill until the cheese is lightly browned, about 2-3 minutes.

~

Chicken Fillet Satay

1½ lb (700 g) chicken breast, off
*   the bone*
4 tablespoons groundnut oil
8 spring onions, cut into ½"
*   (1 cm) pieces*
8 water chestnuts, sliced
1 tablespoon soy sauce
1 tablespoon dry sherry
4 tablespoons satay sauce
chopped coriander leaves or
*   parsley to garnish*

WE HAVE INDONESIA TO THANK FOR THIS DELIGHTFUL DISH WITH ITS SPICY PEANUT (SATAY) SAUCE NOW WIDELY AVAILABLE IN BOTTLES OR JARS. WATER CHESTNUTS, AVAILABLE IN CANS, RETAIN THEIR CRISP TEXTURE THROUGHOUT COOKING.

Skin the chicken and cut into bite-sized pieces. Heat the oil and cook the chicken pieces until done. Then add to the pan the spring onions and water chestnuts and stir-fry for 1 minute. Add the soy sauce, sherry and satay sauce and heat through briskly.

Serve with brown rice, and garnish with chopped coriander or parsley.

~

SERVES 2

4 oz (110 g) chicken breast, off the bone
2 tablespoons oil
1 onion, finely chopped
1 clove garlic, finely chopped
small piece fresh root ginger, finely chopped
4 oz (110 g) cauliflower broken into small florets
4 oz (110 g) mushrooms, thinly sliced
½ red pepper, de-seeded and sliced
1 teaspoon cornflour
1 tablespoon oyster sauce
4 oz (110 g) chicken livers, sliced
4 oz (110 g) beansprouts
salt and pepper
1 tablespoon dry sherry
1½ oz (40 g) cashew nuts, roasted light brown

Chicken for Two

YOU HAVE TO PLAN AHEAD A LITTLE FOR THIS DISH BUT ONCE EVERY-THING IS ASSEMBLED IT'S QUICK TO COOK AND THE COMBINATION OF CHICKEN BREAST AND LIVER WORKS VERY WELL.

Skin the chicken and cut into bite-sized pieces.

Heat the oil in a large frying pan or wok and stir-fry the onion, garlic and root ginger for a minute or two. Add the chicken and continue to stir-fry for a further 2 minutes. Next add the cauli-flower, mushrooms and red pepper and continue to cook for another 2-3 minutes.

In a small bowl mix together the cornflour and the oyster sauce, and when well blended add to the pan, followed by the chicken livers and cook for 2 minutes. Then add the beansprouts and stir-fry for a further 1 minute. Season to taste and then quickly stir in the sherry and cashew nuts.

Serve at once with rice.

~

SERVES 2

2 breasts of chicken, off the bone
1 oz (25 g) butter
1 medium onion, chopped
1 clove garlic, crushed
salt and freshly ground black pepper
2 heads chicory (Belgian endive) or 6 Chinese leaves
2 oz (50 g) walnuts
1 teaspoon caster sugar
2 oz (50 g) Parmesan cheese, grated

Chicken Sorrento

PERFECT FOR ANY OCCASION, THIS DISH IS FAIRLY LIGHT, VERY TASTY AND JUST THAT LITTLE BIT DIFFERENT WITH THE WALNUTS AND PAR-MESAN ADDING SPECIAL INTEREST.

Remove the skin from the chicken breasts and cut the meat into small pieces.

Melt the butter in a pan and cook the onion and garlic together gently for about 5 minutes. Then add the chicken pieces to the pan, season with salt and pepper. Cover and allow to simmer gently for about 5 minutes. Roughly slice the chicory, or Chinese leaves, and add these to the pan, stirring in well with the walnuts and the teaspoon of caster sugar.

Cook for a further minute, stirring occasionally.

Serve on a bed of noodles, sprinkled with Parmesan cheese.

China Chicken with Almonds

*1½ lb (700 g) chicken breast, off
the bone
salt
1½ tablespoons sherry
1½ tablespoons soy sauce
1½ tablespoons cornflour
3 tablespoons water
3 tablespoons oil
1" (2.5 cm) piece of fresh or
stem ginger, finely sliced
6 oz (175 g) frozen peas,
partially thawed
9 spring onions, finely chopped
3 oz (75 g) flaked almonds*

STRICTLY SPEAKING, RICE WINE IS THE AUTHENTIC ALCOHOL INGREDIENT FOR MOST CHINESE STYLE RECIPES BUT IT'S A COMMODITY I, LIKE MOST PEOPLE, RARELY HAVE IN STOCK. SHERRY, PREFERABLY DRY, IS THE STANDARD WESTERN SUBSTITUTE AND WORKS VERY WELL. PLEASE DON'T USE GROUND GINGER IN PLACE OF FRESH – IT'S NOT AS GOOD – ALTHOUGH AS I SUGGEST, A PIECE OF STEM GINGER IS A GOOD SUBSTITUTE.

Skin the chicken breasts and cut into thin, bite-sized strips. Place the strips in a bowl, then season with some salt. Add the sherry and soy sauce and mix through.

In another bowl blend the cornflour with the water and add this to the chicken mixture.

Heat the oil in a large pan or wok until very hot. Add the chicken mixture and cook, stirring all the time, for about 3-4 minutes. Then add the ginger, peas, and spring onions, including some of the green part, and cook for another minute. Throw on the flaked almonds and stir through.

Serve immediately with noodles or rice.

~

China Glaze Chicken

*4 chicken legs
1 oz (25 g) flour
salt and pepper
1 dessertspoon oil
4 oz (110 g) butter
4 tablespoons hoisin sauce
2 teaspoons sugar
juice of 1 lemon
2 teaspoons marjoram
½ teaspoon paprika*

ONE OF THE BEST KNOWN CHINESE BOTTLED SAUCES, HOISIN, WHICH IS SOY BASED, ADDS SHINE AND EXTRA SUCCULENCE TO THIS DISH. IT'S WIDELY AVAILABLE AND CAN BE USED AS A CONDIMENT ALTHOUGH I PREFER IT AS A COOKING INGREDIENT.

Coat the chicken legs with the flour, seasoned with salt and pepper.

In a pan heat the oil with 2 oz (50 g) of the butter. When hot, fry the chicken legs until lightly browned on all sides. Transfer to a shallow ovenproof dish.

In a saucepan melt the other 2 oz (50 g) butter, then add the hoisin sauce, sugar, lemon juice, marjoram and paprika. Stir well together and then spoon all over the chicken.

Bake in the oven at 375°F-190°C-Gas Mark 5 for 50-60 minutes. Baste occasionally during cooking.

Cold Chicken Cromer

Party dish for 6

1 lb (450 g) chicken
4 oz (110 g) flaked almonds
5 fl oz (150 ml) mayonnaise
5 fl oz (150 ml) natural yoghurt
8 oz (225 g) crabmeat, brown
or white
salt and freshly ground white
pepper
1 teaspoon Worcestershire sauce
2 dashes of Tabasco
2 teaspoons tomato purée
5 fl oz (150 ml) double cream,
whipped
salad leaves
chopped parsley to garnish

CROMER IN NORFOLK IS JUSTLY FAMOUS FOR ITS CRAB WHICH, LIKE MOST SHELLFISH, COMBINES VERY SUCCESSFULLY WITH CHICKEN. IF PREFERRED, ALL WHITE CRABMEAT CAN BE USED AND, IF NECESSARY, FROZEN OR CANNED WILL DO AT A PINCH.

Either roast the chicken meat or fry gently in a little butter until cooked. Remove all skin and bones and leave to cool.

Place the flaked almonds on a baking tray and 'toast' them in the oven until lightly browned. Keep to one side.

When cool, cut the chicken into cubes and place in a large mixing bowl. Fold in the mayonnaise with the yoghurt and crabmeat. Season well with salt and pepper. Stir in the Worcestershire sauce and the Tabasco, the tomato purée and whipped cream. Season again to taste.

Arrange the salad leaves on a large serving dish and pile on the chicken mixture. Sprinkle all over with the browned almonds and finely chopped parsley.

~

Cream Bean Chicken

Serves 4

4 chicken pieces, skinned
1 dessertspoon oil
2 oz (50 g) butter
2 medium onions, sliced
1 green pepper, de-seeded and
sliced
1 tablespoon mild chilli powder
(or paprika)
½ pint (275 ml) chicken stock
2 tablespoons tomato purée
8 oz (225 g) can tomatoes
2 teaspoons marjoram or
oregano
1 teaspoon sugar
salt and pepper
8 oz (225 g) can cannellini or
flageolet beans
5 fl oz (150 ml) soured cream
chopped parsley to garnish

A GOOD SUBSTANTIAL MEAL HERE WITH EVERYTHING TO PLEASE THE HEARTY APPETITE.

Preheat the oven to 350°F-180°C-Gas Mark 4.

Heat the oil and butter together and then fry the chicken pieces until brown. Remove from the pan to an ovenproof casserole.

In the same pan gently sauté the onions and the green pepper until soft. Stir in the chilli powder or paprika and cook together for a couple of minutes. Then stir in the stock, tomato purée, canned tomatoes with their liquid, marjoram or oregano, sugar and salt and pepper to taste. Bring to the boil and then pour over the chicken pieces. Cover and cook in the oven for 1 hour.

After that time gently stir in the cannellini or flageolet beans and return to the oven for a further 15 minutes.

When cooked, place on a warm serving dish, pour over the soured cream, sprinkle with chopped parsley and serve.

~

Crusty Chicken Bake

8 chicken pieces
4 fl oz (110 ml) soy sauce
2 tablespoons oil
1 fat clove garlic, chopped
4 tablespoons wheatgerm
4 tablespoons fine dry
*   breadcrumbs*
2 tablespoons sesame seeds
2 tablespoons parsley, chopped
½ teaspoon pepper
½ teaspoon paprika

THERE'S A GENTLE HINT OF THE ORIENT IN THIS DISH, FROM THE SOY SAUCE MARINADE, AND THE LONGER YOU CAN LEAVE THE CHICKEN PIECES IN IT, THE BETTER THE END RESULT.

PRICKING THE CHICKEN PIECES IN SEVERAL PLACES WITH A SHARP-PRONGED CARVING FORK OR SMALL KNIFE WILL HELP THE FLAVOURS IN THE MARINADE TO PENETRATE THE MEAT.

Skin the chicken pieces, if preferred, and prick them all over with a sharp knife. Place them in a shallow dish.

In a small bowl, combine the soy sauce, oil and garlic, and pour over the chicken pieces. Allow the chicken to stand for 20 minutes or longer, turning the pieces once or twice in the marinade.

Meanwhile, mix together the wheatgerm, breadcrumbs, sesame seeds, parsley, pepper and paprika.

Lift the chicken pieces out of the marinade and coat each one in the wheatgerm and breadcrumb mixture.

Place on a buttered baking tray or shallow roasting tin, and bake in the oven at 375°F-190°C-Gas Mark 5 for 40-50 minutes until nicely browned.

~

Headline Chicken

1½ lb (700 g) cooked breast of
*   chicken, off the bone*
1 tablespoon oil
1 medium onion, finely chopped
1 tablespoon curry powder
5 fl oz (150 ml) dry white wine
2 teaspoons tomato purée
juice of ½ lemon
2 tablespoons apricot jam
2 teaspoons cornflour
2 tablespoons water
2 teaspoons tarragon, finely
*   chopped*
½ pint (275 ml) mayonnaise
salad leaves
chopped parsley to garnish

THIS KIND OF DISH IS ALWAYS WELCOME AT A SUMMER LUNCHEON OR ON THE BUFFET TABLE. THE LITTLE EXTRA TIME TAKEN FOR PREPARATION IS WELL REPAID IN THE EATING ENJOYMENT COMPARED TO, SAY, THE STANDARD CHICKEN MAYONNAISE.

Cut the cooked chicken into bite-sized pieces and keep to one side.

In a pan heat the oil and gently cook the onion until soft. Then add to the pan the curry powder, stirring for a moment before adding the wine, tomato purée, lemon juice and apricot jam.

Mix the cornflour with the water and then stir into the pan with the chopped tarragon. Bring everything to the boil and then simmer gently for 10 minutes.

Allow to cool and stir in the mayonnaise. Add the chicken pieces and mix well in the dressing. Place a bed of salad leaves on to a serving dish and pile on the chicken. Sprinkle with chopped parsley.

Herb and Honey Chicken Pieces

SERVES 4

3 tablespoons clear honey
6 tablespoons dried
    breadcrumbs
4 teaspoons fresh mixed herbs,
    chopped
1 teaspoon salt
½ teaspoon pepper
pinch cayenne
8 chicken pieces

THESE PIECES OF CHICKEN BAKED WITH HONEY, HERBS AND FRESH BREADCRUMBS ARE VERY EASY TO MAKE. IF YOU WISH THE CHICKEN CAN BE SKINNED BEFORE COATING, ALTHOUGH I PREFER TO LEAVE THE SKIN ON AND IGNORE THE EXTRA CALORIES.

Preheat the oven to 375°F-190°C-Gas Mark 5.

Place the honey in a shallow dish. (If very stiff warm gently.) In another shallow dish mix together the breadcrumbs, herbs, salt, pepper and cayenne.

Take each chicken piece in turn and roll it first in the honey and then in the seasoned crumbs. Place gently on a baking sheet side by side.

Cook the chicken in the preheated oven for 25 minutes if the chicken is boneless, or for 40 minutes if on the bone.

~

Herb Baked Chicken

SERVES 4

3½ lb (1½ kg) oven-ready
    chicken
6 oz (175 g) carrots, sliced
    thinly
4 oz (110 g) onions, sliced
    thinly
8 fl oz (225 ml) chicken stock
2 tablespoons lemon juice
½ teaspoon rosemary
½ teaspoon thyme
½ teaspoon marjoram
1 teaspoon salt
¼ teaspoon freshly ground
    pepper
chopped parsley to garnish

THIS IS A PARTICULARLY HEALTHY DISH BECAUSE THERE'S NO ADDED FAT. IF YOU WANT TO CUT DOWN ON THE FAT EVEN MORE, YOU CAN SKIN THE CHICKEN PIECES BEFORE BAKING.

Preheat the oven to 325°F-170°C-Gas Mark 3.

Cut the chicken into either 4 or 8 pieces.

In a shallow baking or uncovered casserole dish place a layer of carrots, topped with a layer of sliced onions. Place the chicken pieces, skinside up, on top of the vegetables and pour 4 fl oz (110 ml) of stock over the chicken. Cover tightly, and bake in the oven for 45 minutes.

Meanwhile, in a small saucepan put the remaining stock, lemon juice, rosemary, thyme, marjoram, salt and pepper and bring to the boil. Remove from the heat. Uncover the chicken and pour over the herb stock.

Return the uncovered casserole to the oven, increasing the temperature to 400°F-200°C-Gas Mark 6, and cook for a further 20 minutes, basting the chicken liberally with the herb mixture until the chicken is tender and the skin lightly browned.

To serve, simply spoon the vegetables and pan juices over the chicken and garnish with parsley.

Indian Chicken

8 chicken drumsticks or 4 legs, halved
½ oz (10 g) fresh ginger, grated
½ teaspoon salt
2 teaspoons paprika
1 teaspoon chilli powder
2 cloves garlic, crushed
2 tablespoons lemon juice
4 tablespoons runny honey
2 oz (50 g) butter, melted
chopped coriander leaves to garnish
juice of ½ lemon

ALTHOUGH THIS TITLE SUGGESTS SOMETHING WITH A CURRY FLAVOUR IT ISN'T THE CASE. THE GARLIC, GINGER AND CHILLI COMBINATION, HOWEVER, PROMISE A VERY ENJOYABLE EATING EXPERIENCE.

Pat dry the chicken pieces and prick all over with a sharp knife, and place in a dish.

Next, mix the ginger, salt, paprika and chilli powder together in a bowl. Then add the crushed garlic, lemon juice and honey. Melt the butter and pour over the other ingredients, mixing everything very well together. When well mixed pour over the chicken pieces, and allow to marinate for at least 30 minutes.

When ready to cook, lay the chicken on a rack in a roasting tin, and spoon the marinade over the chicken pieces. Bake in the oven at 400°F-200°C-Gas Mark 6 for about 40 minutes.

Garnish with chopped coriander leaves or parsley and sprinkle over the juice of half a lemon.

~

Japanese Gingered Chicken

1½ lb (700 g) breast of chicken, off the bone
1 tablespoon flour
1" (2.5 cm) piece fresh or stem ginger, finely sliced
4 tablespoons oil
1 onion, sliced
1 red pepper
10 oz (275 g) can bamboo shoots
¼ pint (150 ml) chicken stock
3 tablespoons soy sauce
3 tablespoons dry sherry
salt and pepper
4 oz (100 g) mushrooms, sliced

A PLEASING, COLOURFUL MIXTURE HERE, WITH SHERRY, GINGER AND SOY SAUCE TO BOOST THE INGREDIENTS' FLAVOURS. AS FAR AS SOY SAUCE IS CONCERNED I ALWAYS USE AND RECOMMEND THE KIKKOMAN BRAND FROM JAPAN. IT'S NATURALLY BREWED AND BY FAR THE BEST QUALITY I'VE FOUND.

Remove the skin from the chicken breasts and cut the meat into chunks.

In a bowl mix the flour with the ginger and then coat the chicken pieces with the mixture.

Heat the oil in a large flameproof casserole and fry the chicken with the sliced onion until golden.

De-seed and slice the red pepper and drain the bamboo shoots, and then cut into ½" (1 cm) strips. Add these to the casserole. Stir well and then add the stock, soy sauce and sherry, with some salt and pepper to taste, if required.

Bring to the boil, cover and simmer for 15 minutes. Then add the sliced mushrooms and cook for a further 5-10 minutes.

Serve on a bed of freshly cooked noodles.

Lemon Sunshine Chicken

Serves 4

3 oz (75 g) sultanas
2 tablespoons brandy
2 tablespoons hot water
2 tablespoons oil
3 oz (75 g) butter
4 chicken portions
6 oz (175 g) shallots or onions,
  chopped
grated zest and juice of 1 lemon
salt and pepper
chopped parsley to garnish

I'M NOT A GREAT FAN OF FRUIT IN COOKED SAVOURY DISHES BUT THIS IS AN EXCEPTION AND THE LEMON GIVES IT JUST THE RIGHT CONTRAST.

In a bowl cover the sultanas with the brandy and hot water and leave them to soak for about 1 hour before you are ready to cook.

In a large flameproof casserole dish, heat the oil and butter together and when hot gently brown the chicken pieces on all sides. Remove the chicken to a warm place and cook the shallots or onions in the pan, until they are soft – about 5 minutes.

Return the chicken pieces to the casserole on top of the onions. Add the sultanas with their liquid, the lemon zest and juice, salt and pepper.

Cover and simmer gently for about 45 minutes.

Serve garnished with chopped parsley.

~

Lisbon Chicken

Serves 4

3½ lb (1½ kg) chicken, skinned
  and cut into 8 pieces
¼ pint (150 ml) red wine
2 onions, chopped
2 cloves garlic, crushed
2 bay leaves
2 oz (50 g) dripping
2 oz (50 g) plain flour
1 pint (570 ml) chicken stock
1 tablespoon tomato purée
salt and pepper
2 tablespoons tarragon, chopped
4 tablespoons Port
chopped parsley to garnish

THE LATE ADDITION OF PORT TO THIS DISH GIVES 'DINNER PARTY' STATUS TO WHAT IS, IN ITS OWN RIGHT, A VERY GOOD CASSEROLE SUITABLE FOR ANY OCCASION.

Place the chicken pieces in a bowl and add the red wine. Add to the bowl the onions, garlic and bay leaves. Leave overnight, if possible, or for at least 3 hours, to marinate.

Remove the chicken from the marinade and pat dry. Keep the liquid.

Melt the dripping in a flameproof casserole dish and fry the chicken pieces until lightly browned all over. Sprinkle in the flour and continue to cook, stirring until well dissolved. Stir in the wine marinade, stock, tomato purée, salt and pepper to taste and the tarragon. Cover and bring to the boil, and then simmer for about 1 hour.

Ten minutes before serving, stir in the 4 tablespoons of Port. Adjust the seasoning to taste, sprinkle on some chopped parsley and serve straight from the pot, remembering to remove the bay leaves.

~

Melon Cup Chicken Salad

SERVES 4

1½ lb (700 g) chicken breast
chicken stock to cover, (approx
½ pint/275 ml)
2 ribs celery, thinly sliced
6 oz (175 g) sliced almonds
6 oz (175 g) dried apricots,
soaked overnight and chopped
5 fl oz (150 ml) soured cream
5 fl oz (150 ml) mayonnaise
1½ tablespoons preserved stem
ginger, finely chopped
juice of ½ lemon
½ teaspoon salt
1 teaspoon grated orange peel
pinch of ground nutmeg
2 melons, halved with the seeds
removed (optional)
salad leaves (optional)

THIS IS JUST THE THING FOR A GLAMOROUS SOCIAL OCCASION, ESPE-
CIALLY IF YOU'RE PLANNING TO EAT OUT OF DOORS.

Place the chicken breasts in a saucepan, cover with stock, and simmer gently for 20 minutes. Allow to cool. Cut the chicken into bite-sized pieces, discarding any bones.

In a large bowl combine the chicken pieces, celery, almonds, and chopped apricots.

In a smaller bowl combine the soured cream with the mayonnaise, ginger, lemon juice, salt, orange peel and nutmeg.

Mix just enough of the dressing into the chicken mixture to bind. Reserve the remaining dressing to serve separately. Chill the chicken and dressing for 30 minutes and then serve in the melon halves or, for a simpler presentation, heap the chicken on a bed of salad leaves.

~

Sweet and Spicy Chicken

SERVES 4

8 chicken pieces

for the sweet marinade
2 oz (50 g) butter, melted
1 level teaspoon ground ginger
grated zest of 1 orange
juice of 1 orange
1 tablespoon honey

for the spicy marinade
2-3 tablespoons oil
1 teaspoon curry powder or
paste
2 cloves garlic, crushed
1 teaspoon made mustard,
either French or English
juice of ½ lemon

THERE IS TWICE THE EATING PLEASURE HERE IF YOU ALLOW A PIECE
OF CHICKEN WITH EACH KIND OF COATING PER PERSON, OR, IF YOU
LIKE, JUST ONE METHOD CAN BE USED BY DOUBLING THE FLAVOURING
INGREDIENTS. PLAIN BOILED NOODLES OR SAUTÉ POTATOES WITH A
SIMPLE SALAD MAKE IDEAL ACCOMPANIMENTS.

Preheat the oven to 400°F-200°C-Gas Mark 6.

Blend all the ingredients for both marinades in separate dishes and marinade 4 chicken pieces in each dish, making sure the chicken pieces are well coated. Marinade for 3 hours, or overnight if possible.

Using two separate ovenproof dishes place the sweet chicken pieces in one and the spicy chicken pieces in the other with their marinades. Bake in the oven for about 20-25 minutes and remember to baste the chicken a couple of times during cooking.

~

Whisky Chicken

SERVES 4

4 chicken breasts, boneless
1 tablespoon oil
1 oz (25 g) butter
1 medium onion, finely chopped
1 teaspoon curry powder
grated zest of 1 orange
1 measure whisky
*salt and freshly ground black
    pepper*
5 fl oz (150 ml) double cream

to garnish
1 oz (25 g) butter
2 oz (50 g) flaked almonds
orange segments

ORIGINALLY PASSED ON TO ME BY A GOOD FRIEND, I'VE GIVEN THIS DISH LITERALLY TO HUNDREDS OF PEOPLE AT MY SUMMER COUNTY ROADSHOW DEMONSTRATIONS AND IT'S PERFECTLY TRUE TO SAY THEY ALL WANTED MORE. IT'S A REAL WINNER.

Cut the chicken into bite-sized pieces.

Heat the oil and butter in a pan. Add the onion with the curry powder and cook gently, stirring, for 3-4 minutes. Add the chicken pieces with the orange zest and the whisky, and salt and pepper to taste.

Keep the pan contents on the move until the chicken is cooked through. Stir in the cream and blend through well. Heat gently until the sauce has thickened slightly.

Melt the butter in a small pan and brown the almonds in it.

Serve the chicken on a heated dish topped with the flaked almonds, and surrounded with orange segments.

~

L A M B

8 lamb kidneys
¼ pint (150 ml) chicken stock
salt and freshly ground black
*   pepper*
1 tablespoon oil
1 medium onion, thinly sliced
1 red pepper, cored, de-seeded
*   and sliced*
1 green pepper, cored, de-seeded
*   and sliced*
1 clove garlic, crushed
15 oz (425 g) can red kidney
*   beans, drained*
2 tomatoes, sliced
7 fl oz (200 ml) natural yoghurt
2 eggs
2 oz (50 g) Cheddar cheese,
*   grated*

Bean, Kidney and Pepper Bake

THE HIGH FOOD VALUE OF KIDNEYS AND OTHER OFFAL MEATS IS WELL DOCUMENTED. EVEN SO, A CERTAIN AMOUNT OF PERSUASION IS OFTEN REQUIRED AT THE FAMILY TABLE. THIS COLOURFUL RECIPE SHOULD PROVIDE ALL THE INTEREST AND ENCOURAGEMENT NECESSARY FOR EVERYONE'S SATISFACTION.

Skin the kidneys, remove the core carefully and slice. Put the kidneys into a shallow pan with the chicken stock and salt and pepper and simmer gently for about 5-6 minutes until the kidneys are just tender.

In another pan heat the oil and fry the onions gently for 3-4 minutes. Add the sliced red and green peppers and the garlic. Cover the pan and cook gently for 5 minutes. Drain the kidneys and mix in with the peppers and onion. Stir in the drained kidney beans and heat through. Spoon the mixture into a greased, shallow gratin dish. Arrange the slices of tomato over the top.

In a bowl beat the yoghurt with the eggs and seasoning and spoon evenly over the vegetables, beans and kidneys. Sprinkle the top with the grated cheese and bake in the oven at 375°F-190°C-Gas Mark 5 for about 30 minutes, until the yoghurt topping is golden and set.

~

SERVES 4

SERVES 4

4 small lamb chops
4 small pork chops
1 tablespoon oil
2 medium onions
2 large tomatoes
2 medium potatoes
1 medium green pepper
2 oz (50 g) long-grain rice
salt and pepper
1 teaspoon basil, chopped
2 teaspoons thyme, chopped
1 pint (570 ml) chicken stock
4 oz (110 g) Cheddar cheese,
   grated

Canadian Pork and Lamb

As I recall it was a friendly Canadian couple I knew in my bachelor days who first introduced me to this combination casserole. The memory of their kindness and the dish itself have never left me. One small point, if fresh basil is unavailable then please don't use dried. Half a teaspoon of tarragon is a perfect substitute.

Trim the fat from the chops. Heat the oil in a heavy pan and fry the chops on both sides until browned.

Peel and slice the onions and potatoes. Slice the tomatoes. Core and de-seed the green pepper and cut into narrow strips.

In the bottom of a 1 pint (570 ml) casserole dish arrange a layer of one third of the onions, tomatoes, potatoes and green pepper. Place the lamb chops on the top of the vegetable layer. Sprinkle with salt, pepper, basil and thyme. Add another layer of a third of the vegetables and arrange the pork chops on the top. Sprinkle with the rice, salt, pepper, basil and thyme. Top with the remaining vegetables and seasoning.

Pour on the stock, cover and bake in the oven at 350°F-180°C-Gas Mark 4 for 1½ hours, or until the meat and vegetables are tender.

After 1½ hours, remove the cover, sprinkle with the grated cheese and return to the oven for just about 5-10 minutes, or until the cheese has melted.

~

SERVES 4

2 tablespoons oil
4 good sized lamb chops
1 large onion, sliced
*1 small green pepper, cored, de-
seeded and cut into strips*
3 oz (75 g) mushrooms, sliced
*7 fl oz (200 ml) stock mixed
with 2-3 tablespoons lemon
juice*
pinch of dried rosemary
salt and freshly ground pepper
¼ pint (150 ml) soured cream
grated zest of ½ lemon
chopped parsley to garnish

Citrus Lamb Casserole

THERE'S A CREAMY, LEMONY ELEGANCE ABOUT THIS RECIPE WHICH IS
PERFECT SERVED ON A BED OF GREEN NOODLES OR TAGLIATELLI.

Preheat the oven to 350°F-180°C-Gas Mark 4.

Heat the oil in a flameproof casserole and fry the chops until
browned. Remove from the casserole.

Fry the onions in the remaining oil until soft. Then add the
green pepper and mushrooms and fry for three more minutes.

Return the chops to the casserole with the stock and lemon juice
mixture, rosemary, salt and pepper to taste. Cover and cook in the
oven for 1 hour.

Remove from the oven. Mix together the soured cream and
lemon zest and add to the casserole, stirring well. Adjust the seasoning and serve garnished with chopped parsley.

~

SERVES 4

*1¾ lb (800 g) lean, boneless
lamb*
*2 oz (50 g) Parma ham or
unsmoked back bacon, de-
rinded*
1 small onion
2 stalks celery
2 tablespoons oil
2 oz (50 g) butter
¼ pint (150 ml) dry white wine
*¼ pint (150 ml) chicken stock or
water*
a few parsley stalks
sprig of oregano
black pepper
1 tablespoon lemon juice
2 large egg yolks
2 tablespoons chopped parsley
salt

Coliseum Casserole

ANOTHER TRULY LOVELY DISH FROM ROME, WHERE THE LOCALS
SEEM TO HAVE A REAL GIFT FOR COOKING LAMB. HALF A TEASPOON
OF DRIED OREGANO WILL DO IF YOU CAN'T GET HOLD OF A FRESH
SPRIG.

Cut the lamb into large cubes. Cut the ham or bacon into strips.
Finely chop the onion and celery.

Heat the oil and butter in a large flameproof casserole dish. Add
the lamb and fry until golden on all sides. Remove the meat with a
slotted spoon. Then gently fry the ham or bacon, with the onion
and celery. Return the lamb to the casserole and stir in the wine.
Bring to the boil. Reduce the heat and simmer, uncovered, for
about 10 minutes. Then add the stock or water.

Tie the parsley stalks and oregano together with string and add
the bunch to the pot. Bring back to simmering point, reduce the
heat as low as possible, and cover and cook for 45 minutes, stirring and turning the meat occasionally.

In a cup lightly beat the lemon juice, egg yolks and chopped
parsley. Stir a few spoonfuls of liquid from the casserole dish into
the cup, then stir the contents of the cup into the casserole. Remove from the heat and lift out the bunch of herbs.

Season to taste and serve at once.

Creamy Kidneys

*1 lb (450 g) lamb or veal
   kidneys*
salt and pepper
½ teaspoon paprika
4 oz (110 g) butter
*1½ oz (40 g) onion, finely
   chopped*
3½ fl oz (100 ml) stock
4 oz (110 g) mushrooms, sliced
4 fl oz (110 ml) double cream
dash of vinegar
1 dessertspoon parsley, chopped
1 oz (25 g) horseradish, grated

KIDNEYS, TO ME, ARE A MUCH UNDERRATED DELICACY AND THE HARD, OVERDONE TREATMENT THEY OFTEN RECEIVE REALLY DOESN'T DO THEM JUSTICE. THIS COMBINATION, INCLUDING CREAM AND MUSHROOMS WITH THE CONTRASTING LIGHT SHARPNESS OF VINEGAR AND HORSERADISH, IS WONDERFUL. IF YOU ARE LUCKY ENOUGH TO FIND VEAL KIDNEYS THEY ARE EVEN MORE DELICIOUS.

First prepare the kidneys. Cut out the core, and if necessary peel off the skin. Slice the kidneys in half, lengthways, and season with salt, pepper and paprika.

Melt 1 oz (25 g) of the butter and soften the onion gently. Then add the stock and allow to simmer together over a low heat. Melt the remaining 3 oz (75 g) of butter in a separate pan and cook the kidneys for 4 minutes maximum – even less time would be better. Remove from the pan and keep warm.

Cook the sliced mushrooms in the kidney juices and then drain this cooking liquid into the onion pan. Add the double cream, dash of vinegar, the chopped parsley and horseradish. Stir everything together and heat slowly to just below boiling point – then mix in the kidneys and mushrooms.

This makes a substantial snack on thick toast or butter-fried bread.

~

Dairy Dressed Lamb

AFTER ITS CONVENTIONAL BROWNING, WITH THE SUGAR PROVIDING AN EXTRA EDGE OF CARAMEL, THE LAMB IS GENTLY POACHED IN THE MILK STOCK. IT IS THEN AWAKENED WITH NUTMEG, CREAM AND LEMON AND DRESSED WITH ITS MANTLE OF SOFT FRIED ONION RINGS.

SERVES 4

2 lb (900 g) boned shoulder of
    lamb
1 tablespoon oil
1 tablespoon sugar
1 tablespoon plain flour
1 pint (570 ml) milk
salt and pepper
1 oz (25 g) pearl barley
6 ribs of celery, sliced
1½ oz (40 g) butter
1 large onion, sliced in rings
2 fl oz (50 ml) single cream
juice of ½ lemon
½ teaspoon nutmeg, grated
chopped parsley to garnish

Preheat the oven to 475°F-240°C-Gas Mark 9.

Cut the lamb into chunks. Heat the oil and sugar in a pan and fry the lamb until lightly browned. Drain off the juices and remove the meat to a casserole dish.

Blend the flour with a little of the milk, then add the rest of the milk, season with salt and pepper and pour over the lamb. Add the barley and celery, cover and cook in the oven for 20 minutes. After 20 minutes turn the oven temperature down to 300°F-150°C-Gas Mark 2, and cook for a further 1 hour and 20 minutes.

Melt the butter and fry the onion rings until a light brown colour.

Remove the casserole from the oven. Blend together the cream, lemon juice and nutmeg and stir into the casserole.

Garnish the top with the fried onion rings and chopped parsley.

~

Elizabeth Lamb

SERVES 4

2 lb (900 g) lamb shoulder
2 large onions
3 large tomatoes
2 cloves garlic (optional)
large handful of mint leaves
1 pint light stock
salt and freshly ground black
    pepper
juice of 1 lemon

MY FIRST JOB IN BROADCASTING TOOK ME TO LIVE IN WALES AND BROWSING IN CARDIFF CITY LIBRARY ONE DAY, I LEARNED THAT THE CUSTOM OF SERVING MINT SAUCE WITH LAMB COMES FROM THE ELIZABETHAN AGE WHEN, IN ORDER TO ENCOURAGE THE CONSUMPTION OF FISH AND TO PROTECT THE WOOL INDUSTRY, HER GRACIOUS MAJESTY, QUEEN ELIZABETH DECREED THAT LAMB COULD ONLY BE EATEN WITH BITTER HERBS. THE LEAST BITTER HERB AVAILABLE THEN, IT SEEMS, WAS MINT AND TODAY WE STILL FOLLOW THE HABIT. PERSONALLY I PREFER THE JELLIED VARIETY WHICH DOESN'T RUN ALL OVER THE PLATE, UNLIKE THE OFTEN TOO VINEGARY SAUCE. THE FRESH CHOPPED MINT LEAVES USED HERE REMOVE THE NECESSITY FOR EITHER KIND.

Trim the lamb of any fat and cut up into pieces.

Slice the onions into rings. Plunge the tomatoes into boiling water for 30 seconds. Remove and peel under the cold tap, then chop them. Crush the garlic, if using. Chop the mint leaves finely.

Place all the above ingredients into a large ovenproof casserole dish. Pour in the stock, and season with salt and pepper.

Bring to the boil on the hob and then cover and place in the oven at 325°F-170°C-Gas Mark 3 for 1½ hours.

Heat the lemon juice in a small saucepan and then add this to the casserole.

Return to the oven and cook for a further ½ hour. (Total cooking time 2 hours.)

~

Extra Irish Stew

AS A DUBLINER, MY CHILDHOOD ENCOUNTERS WITH IRISH STEW WERE ON A VERY SIMPLE LEVEL INDEED AND NO LESS SATISFYING FOR THAT. IT'S A WONDERFUL DISH AND REGARDED BY MANY AS TASTING EVEN BETTER WHEN REHEATED THE DAY AFTER MAKING. THIS RECIPE FEATURES MANY EXTRA INGREDIENTS AND A HIGHER QUALITY CUT OF MEAT AND WILL RECEIVE 'A HUNDRED THOUSAND WELCOMES' FROM ANY COMPANY.

SERVES 4

1½ lb (700 g) lamb fillet or leg steaks
4 oz (110 g) piece bacon, de-rinded
2 tablespoons oil
1 tablespoon flour
2 large onions, cut into chunks or 18 peeled button onions
1 clove garlic, crushed
10 oz (275 g) carrots, diced
1 pint (570 ml) chicken stock
12 oz (350 g) potatoes, peeled and diced
salt and freshly ground black pepper
2 tablespoons chopped parsley and 4 spring onions, finely sliced including some green part to garnish

optional
4-6 tablespoons mashed potato
Worcestershire sauce

Trim the lamb and cut into cubes, and dice the bacon. Heat the oil in a small pan and gently fry the bacon for a few minutes. Remove and transfer to a good sized flameproof casserole dish, placed over a moderate heat. Add the cubed lamb and gently stir-fry the meat for 3-4 minutes. Sprinkle on the flour and stir in well. Add the onions, garlic and diced carrots.

Pour over the chicken stock, cover and cook in the oven at 375°F-190°C-Gas Mark 5 for 1¼ hours, or until the meat is tender. Then add the diced potatoes and cook for a further 20 minutes until they are done. Season to taste.

If you wish to lightly thicken the stew, stir in some mashed potato.

Serve the stew in separate bowls, generously sprinkled with chopped parsley and chopped spring onions.

Worcestershire sauce goes extremely well with this dish.

~

Lamb Stir-fry

SERVES 4

1½ lb (700 g) lean lamb
1 tablespoon flour
salt and pepper
2 oz (50 g) butter
2 tablespoons oil
1 clove garlic, crushed
grated zest of 1 lemon
4 oz (110 g) cucumber, sliced
4 oz (110 g) spring onions,
    chopped, including the green
    part
12 oz (350 g) tomatoes, skinned
    and quartered
juice of 1 lemon

THE CHINESE QUICK COOKING METHOD OF STIR-FRYING DEVELOPED BECAUSE OF A SHORTAGE OF FUEL. GASTRONOMICALLY, IT WAS A HAPPY DEPRIVATION AND RESULTED IN A CRISPER, BRIGHTER TASTE WITH REDUCED LOSS OF VITAMINS. THE SALAD VEGETABLES USED HERE MAKE THIS A PERFECT SUMMER DISH.

Cut the lamb into thin strips, and coat in the flour, seasoned with salt and pepper.

Melt the butter and oil together in a large pan, adding the garlic and lemon zest. Then add the meat, and cook over a fairly high heat for 3-4 minutes, until it is browned.

Remove the lamb and add the sliced cucumber and spring onions to the juices in the pan. Stir-fry for 2 minutes, then return the lamb to the pan with the tomatoes and lemon juice. Continue to stir-fry until warmed through. Season to taste and serve with boiled rice or noodles.

~

Lamb Tagine

SERVES 4

1½ lb (700 g) boned shoulder of
    lamb
1 tablespoon seasoned flour
2 tablespoons oil
1 large onion, sliced
1 green pepper, de-seeded and
    cut into strips
1 head of fennel, sliced
½ pint (275 ml) of chicken stock
½ teaspoon ground ginger
1 packet saffron powder
1 strip orange peel
salt and pepper
3 oz (75 g) dried apricots
1 tablespoon lemon juice

ONE OF THE SO-CALLED CLASSIC ARABIAN DISHES OF WHICH THERE ARE A NUMBER OF VARIATIONS, WHICH IS NOT SURPRISING SINCE TAGINE SIMPLY MEANS POT. THE USE OF FENNEL, SAFFRON AND APRICOTS PROVIDES A DELICIOUS DIFFERENCE, WITHOUT BEING TOO 'EXOTIC'.

Trim the lamb of any fat and cut into cubes. Dust the meat in the seasoned flour and lightly brown in the oil in a flameproof casserole dish.

Remove the lamb to a plate, and gently stir-fry the vegetables for 5 minutes, after which return the meat to the pan and add the stock, ginger, saffron powder, orange peel and salt and pepper. Bring to the boil, cover, and gently simmer on the hob for 1 hour.

Then add the chopped dried apricots and cook for a further 15 minutes.

Just before serving stir in the lemon juice and serve with either boiled rice or couscous.

Lamb with Apricot Sauce

SERVES 6

for the marinade
4 oz (110 g) dried apricots
1 oz (25 g) dripping
2 medium onions, sliced
1 level tablespoon curry powder
1 clove garlic, crushed
juice of 1 lemon
1 oz (25 g) sugar
3 tablespoons wine vinegar
salt and freshly ground black
    pepper

6 lamb leg steaks

THE MAIN ROLE OF THE MARINADE HERE IS TO PROVIDE A DE-LICIOUSLY FRUITY YET SPICY SAUCE FOR THE GRILLED LAMB STEAKS. IF AT ALL POSSIBLE DO PLAN TO PREPARE THIS DISH THE NIGHT BEFORE – IT MAKES THE WHOLE THING EASIER TO COOK NEXT DAY AND THE LONG MARINADING TIME IMPROVES THE FLAVOURS OF BOTH THE SAUCE AND THE MEAT. 'NO NEED TO SOAK' APRICOTS ARE AVAILABLE AT SUPERMARKETS AND SHOULD BE USED HERE.

Cook the apricots in enough water to cover for about 20 minutes. Strain, and then purée them in a food processor or blender.

In a pan melt the dripping and fry the onions gently until soft. Add to the pan the curry powder, stirring in well, the garlic, lemon juice, sugar, vinegar and salt and pepper. Lastly stir through the apricot purée. Simmer everything together very gently for a few minutes. Pour this mixture over the raw lamb steaks and leave to marinade in the refrigerator for at least 3 hours or overnight if possible.

When ready to cook, lift the meat out carefully and grill for 4 minutes on each side.

Heat the apricot sauce, simmering gently until the lamb is cooked. Pour over the meat just before serving.

~

Lemon and Rosemary Lamb Casserole

SERVES 4

4 best end of neck lamb chops
2 tablespoons oil
1 large onion, sliced
1 green pepper, cored, de-seeded
    and cut into strips
3 oz (75 g) mushrooms, sliced
7 fl oz (200 ml) stock
3 tablespoons lemon juice
1 teaspoon rosemary, chopped
salt and freshly ground black
    pepper
5 fl oz (150 ml) soured cream
grated rind of ½ lemon
chopped parsley to garnish

ROSEMARY IS A LOVELY FRAGRANT HERB ALTHOUGH ALWAYS REMEM-BER THE CAREFUL COOK'S MOTTO 'ENOUGH IS ENOUGH'. IT'S A GOOD IDEA TO CHOP IT FINELY FOR COMFORTABLE EATING.

Fry the chops in the oil in a flameproof casserole dish until they are browned. Remove from the dish then fry the onion until soft, add the green pepper strips and the mushrooms and fry for a further 3 minutes.

Return the chops to the casserole dish with the stock mixed with the lemon juice, the rosemary and salt and pepper. Cover and cook in the oven at 350°F-180°C-Gas Mark 4 for 1 hour.

Mix together the soured cream and the lemon rind and add this to the casserole, stirring through well.

Adjust the seasoning and garnish with parsley.

Sweet and Spicy Chicken (page 71) and
Spaghetti alla Carbonara (page 99).

Lemony Lamb

LEMON HAS A GREAT AFFINITY WITH LAMB, ESPECIALLY WHEN COMBINED WITH FRESH HERBS. THE DRY VERMOUTH SUGGESTED HERE CONTAINS, AMONG OTHER HERBS, WORMWOOD, A RELATIVE OF TARRAGON WHICH PROVIDES A SUBTLE FLAVOUR OF THE DISH.

SERVES 4

1½ lb (700 g) boned shoulder or
    leg of lamb
1 oz (25 g) lard
2 oz (50 g) unsmoked gammon,
    chopped
1 onion, chopped
2 tablespoons flour
salt and pepper
4 tablespoons dry vermouth
¾ pint (425 ml) light stock
2 egg yolks
juice of ½ lemon
½ teaspoon finely grated lemon
    rind
1 teaspoon marjoram, chopped
1 tablespoon parsley, chopped

Cut the lamb into 1" (2.5 cm) cubes.

Melt the lard in a heavy pan and add the gammon, lamb cubes and onion and fry gently for 10 minutes, stirring frequently. Sprinkle in the flour and season to taste with salt and pepper. Cook, stirring, for 1 minute.

Add the vermouth, bring to the boil and then add the stock and bring back to the boil, stirring. Cover and simmer for 45 minutes or until the lamb is tender.

Beat together the egg yolks, rind and juice of the lemon and the herbs. Add 3 tablespoons of the cooking liquid and blend well. Add to the pan and stir well to mix in; do not allow to boil. Check the seasoning and serve.

~

Liver with Caramel Orange

A DISH OF CONTRAST AND INTEREST. DON'T WORRY ABOUT THE AMOUNT OF DRY MUSTARD USED. WHEN COOKED MUSTARD ALWAYS LOSES ITS FIERCE HEAT – WHICH IS WHY MUSTARD MUST ALWAYS BE MADE WITH COLD WATER.

SERVES 4

1 lb (450 g) calf's or lamb's
    liver
1 orange
3 oz (75 g) butter
1 oz (25 g) sugar
½ teaspoon salt
1 teaspoon pepper
2 teaspoons dry English
    mustard powder
¼ teaspoon cayenne pepper
3-4 tablespoons flour
1 medium onion, finely chopped
1 large clove garlic, crushed
1 glass red wine
½ glass stock
1 tablespoon mixed chopped
    herbs
sprigs of watercress to garnish

Slice the liver thinly, with a very sharp knife.

Slice the orange, without peeling, and fry in 1 oz (25 g) of butter, dusting well with the sugar in the pan, until nicely coloured. Lift out and keep warm.

Mix the salt and pepper, mustard powder and cayenne with the flour, and dip the liver slices in this mixture.

Heat a large frying pan and drop in 1½ oz (40 g) of butter, and put in the liver and fry quickly on both sides for one minute. Lift on to a hot serving dish and slip into a warm oven.

Add the remaining ½ oz (10 g) of butter to the pan and when melted add the onion and garlic. Sauté for 2 or 3 minutes, then add the wine. Reduce by half, add the stock and herbs. Boil up and spoon over the liver. Garnish with the orange slices and sprigs of watercress, if available. Serve at once.

Salami Salad (page 114), *Janssen's Temptation* (page 106) and
Onion Tart (page 107).

Roman Lamb

SERVES 4

*1½ lb (700 g) boned shoulder or
   leg of lamb*
1 oz (25 g) lard
*salt and freshly ground black
   pepper*
1 clove garlic, crushed
1 teaspoon sage leaves, chopped
2 teaspoons rosemary, chopped
2 teaspoons plain flour
6 tablespoons wine vinegar
6 tablespoons water
3 anchovy fillets, chopped finely

BASED ON A CLASSIC FAVOURITE FROM THE LAZIO REGION OF ITALY AND USUALLY MADE WITH MILK-FED BABY LAMB. THE PERHAPS SURPRISING USE OF ANCHOVY FILLETS IS QUITE AUTHENTIC AND RESULTS IN A SAUCE WHICH IS TRULY DELICIOUSLY DIFFERENT.

Trim any fat from the lamb and cut into 2" (5 cm) cubes.

Melt the lard in a saucepan and brown the lamb cubes all over. Add salt, pepper, garlic, sage and rosemary to the saucepan and stir in.

Sprinkle over the flour and continue to cook, stirring until the flour is absorbed. Add the wine vinegar, bring to the boil and then add the water. Reduce the heat and cover the saucepan, cooking over a low heat for about 1 hour, or until tender. (This should be a gentle simmer.)

Turn the meat occasionally and if necessary add another 2-3 tablespoons of water.

When the meat is cooked, remove 2-3 tablespoons of the sauce into a small bowl. Add the chopped anchovies to this and mash together into a thin paste. Pour this all over the lamb. Turn the lamb again in its sauce, for a further 30 seconds.

Serve with buttered noodles.

~

Splendidly Stuffed Courgettes

ALTHOUGH THIS DISH REQUIRES A LITTLE DETAILED PREPARATION THE ATTRACTIVE APPEARANCE AND LOVELY COMBINATION OF FLAVOURS MAKES IT WELL WORTH THE EFFORT. IT CAN BE SERVED EITHER AS A FIRST COURSE OR AS A LIGHT LUNCHEON DISH WITH SALAD.

SERVES 4

4 fair sized courgettes
2 tomatoes, peeled, de-seeded
    and chopped
2 oz (50 g) small peas, fresh or
    frozen
2 oz (50 g) rice, cooked
½ teaspoon marjoram or
    oregano
1 clove garlic, crushed
salt and pepper
2 tablespoons oil
1 large onion, finely chopped
6 oz (175 g) minced lamb
½ pint (275 ml) stock
4 oz (110 g) Emmenthal cheese,
    grated
1 oz (25 g) butter
chopped parsley to garnish

Preheat the oven to 350°F-180°C-Gas Mark 4.

Wash the courgettes, trim the ends and halve, lengthways. With a teaspoon or apple corer remove the centre flesh from the courgettes and chop finely.

Place the chopped courgette flesh in a large bowl together with the tomatoes, peas, rice, marjoram and garlic. Season with salt and pepper and mix well.

Next, gently heat the oil in a frying pan and cook the onion until soft. Then add the minced lamb and stir-fry until brown. Season with salt and pepper and transfer to the bowl containing the courgette mixture. Combine everything well together.

Arrange the courgette shells in an ovenproof dish, and fill them with the lamb mixture. Pour the stock around the courgettes, cover the dish and place in the oven for 25 minutes.

Remove from the oven, sprinkle on the grated cheese and dot with butter. Return to the oven, uncovered, for 10 minutes until the cheese has melted. Garnish with chopped parsley.

~

Stuffed Aubergines

2 good sized aubergines
oil to deep fry
10 oz (275 g) minced lamb, beef
    or sausagemeat
1 clove of garlic, crushed
salt and pepper
3 tablespoons fresh breadcrumbs
1 tablespoon parsley, chopped
1 tablespoon Parmesan cheese,
    grated (optional)
1-2 oz (25-50 g) butter

ALSO REFERRED TO AS THE EGG PLANT BECAUSE OF THE SHAPE OF SOME OF ITS VARIETIES, THE GENTLE EARTHY FLAVOUR OF THE AUBERGINE PROVIDES A PERFECT BACKGROUND FOR ANY TYPE OF MINCED MEAT. ITS SKIN ALSO PROVIDES AN EXCELLENT NATURAL CONTAINER FOR THIS STRAIGHTFORWARD MIXTURE.

Preheat the oven to 350°F-180°C-Gas Mark 4.

Slice the aubergines in half lengthways and score the flesh with a sharp knife, taking care not to break the skins. Deep fry for 2-3 minutes, remove from the oil and drain on kitchen paper. Scoop out the pulp with a spoon. Mix the chopped aubergine pulp with the meat, crushed garlic and salt and pepper.

Place the aubergine shells in an oiled baking dish and fill them with the meat mixture.

Mix together the breadcrumbs, parsley and cheese and sprinkle over the stuffed aubergines. Dot the tops with small flecks of butter and bake in the oven for 30 minutes.

~

Suffolk Stew

3 oz (75 g) dried lentils
3 tablespoons dried haricot
    beans
3 tablespoons barley
2 large potatoes, peeled and
    chopped roughly
1 large turnip or swede,
    chopped roughly
4 carrots, peeled and chopped
    roughly
4 onions, peeled and chopped
    roughly
4 good thick lamb chops
2 bay leaves
½ teaspoon salt
½ teaspoon pepper
1 clove garlic, crushed
1 teaspoon mixed herbs
4 pints (2¼ litres) water
1 tablespoon Worcestershire
    sauce (optional)

THE FIRST ESSENTIAL REQUIREMENT FOR THIS DISH IS A VERY HEARTY APPETITE. THE STRAIGHTFORWARD GOODNESS OF ITS SIMPLE INGREDIENTS IS SELF EVIDENT. GROWING TEENAGERS AND STUDENTS WILL ESPECIALLY LOVE IT.

Soak the lentils, haricot beans and barley overnight in cold water. When ready to cook the stew, strain the pulses, discarding the liquid.

Place all the chopped vegetables in a large saucepan, then add the chops together with the bay leaves, salt and pepper, garlic and herbs. Next add the lentils, beans and barley to the pot, pour over 4 pints (2¼ litres) of water, and the Worcestershire sauce, if used.

Bring to the boil and boil rapidly for at least 10 minutes, cover with a lid and simmer gently for 3 hours.

~

Taj Mahal Treat

SERVES 4

1 lb (450 g) lamb or calf's liver
10 fl oz (275 ml) natural
    yoghurt
4 oz (110 g) butter
3 teaspoons oil
2 large onions, chopped
2 cloves garlic, crushed
2 dessertspoons curry powder
1 teaspoon ground ginger
pinch of cayenne pepper
3 tomatoes, skinned and
    chopped
salt

A VERY APPETISING DISH WHICH OFFERS HIGH QUALITY NOURISH-MENT AND A MEMORABLE SPICY FLAVOUR.

With a sharp knife, cut the liver into thin strips. In a bowl, toss the liver with the yoghurt to coat, and if possible leave for 30 minutes to 1 hour.

Melt half the butter in a pan with half the oil and gently cook the onions and garlic until soft. Sprinkle with the curry powder, ginger and cayenne pepper. Mix well and add the tomatoes and a little salt to taste. Cook for 5 minutes. Drain the yoghurt into the pan, mix in and continue to cook gently.

Meanwhile, in another pan melt the rest of the butter with the rest of the oil and stir-fry the liver strips until cooked as liked. Add the liver to the curry sauce, mix well and serve with boiled rice.

~

Tarragon Meatballs

SERVES 4

1 lb (450 g) lamb, minced
salt and black pepper
2 oz (50 g) white breadcrumbs
1 egg, beaten
1 tablespoon oil
1 oz (25 g) butter
1 onion, chopped
2 sticks celery, chopped
2 carrots, sliced
2 tablespoons tarragon, chopped
2 tablespoons clear honey
1 tablespoon cider vinegar
½ pint (275 ml) dry cider

TARRAGON RATES VERY HIGHLY ON THE ESSENTIAL LIST OF HERBS AND THE FRENCH VARIETY IS THE ONLY ONE TO USE FOR COOKING. ITS FLAVOUR IS DIFFICULT TO DESCRIBE, ALTHOUGH 'RACY' AND 'PUNGENT' HAVE BOTH BEEN USED. IT IS A GREAT HERB, AS THIS RECIPE WILL EASILY CONVINCE YOU.

Put the minced lamb into a bowl, and season with salt and pepper. Mix in the breadcrumbs and then the beaten egg. Stir well. Take spoonfuls of the mixture and shape into balls – about the size of a golf ball.

In a saucepan heat the oil and butter together and then brown the meatballs on all sides. Remove from the pan with a slotted spoon. Add the vegetables to the pan and cook them gently until soft. Add the tarragon, honey, cider vinegar and cider and bring to the boil. Return the meatballs to the pan and simmer gently, covered, for about 30 minutes.

Serve with mashed potatoes.

~

Quite a number of people, I've found, especially those living in towns and cities, are rather nervous about cooking pheasant, although nothing could be simpler. After all, it's just another bird which only needs a few rashers of streaky bacon laid over the breast to keep it from getting overdone and some seasoning and a knob of butter in the cavity.

Preheat the oven to 375°F-190°C-Gas Mark 5 and roast for about 45 minutes, basting occasionally, and remove the bacon for the last 10 minutes of cooking time to allow the breast to brown. I serve the breast and thighs only, as the drumsticks can be a bit stringy.

The following two pheasant recipes are both very good and are ideal for entertaining, since there's no need to carve after cooking.

PHEASANT

1 pheasant
1 tablespoon oil
1 oz (25 g) butter
12 oz (350 g) chestnuts, shelled
8 oz (225 g) small white onions
  or shallots
1 tablespoon flour
1 pint (570 ml) chicken stock
grated zest and juice of 1 orange
2 dessertspoons redcurrant jelly
1 glass red wine
bouquet garni
salt and pepper
chopped parsley to garnish

Chestnut Pheasant

Cut the pheasant into quarters.

Heat the oil and butter together in a flameproof casserole dish and brown the pheasant pieces all over. Remove from the pan.

Stir in the chestnuts and the onions and stir-fry until they begin to brown. Add the flour to the casserole and mix in well. Add all the remaining ingredients, except the parsley, and bring to the boil. Return the pheasant to the casserole and cover tightly. Cook in the oven at 325°F-170°C-Gas Mark 3 for 1-1½ hours.

When cooked, remove the bouquet garni, add seasoning to taste and serve garnished with chopped parsley.

~

2 small pheasant
2 tablespoons oil
2 oz (50 g) butter
juice of 1 lemon
2 sprigs rosemary, finely
  chopped
2 sprigs thyme, finely chopped
salt and freshly ground black
  pepper
3 cooking apples, peeled, cored
  and sliced
10 fl oz (275 ml) cider
5 fl oz (150 ml) double cream
½ teaspoon cinnamon
chopped parsley to garnish

Pheasants in Cider

Take the pheasants and split them in two, lengthways.

In a flameproof casserole dish melt 1 tablespoon oil with 1 oz (25 g) butter and brown the pheasants all over. Remove from the casserole dish to a plate and sprinkle the insides of the birds with lemon juice, rosemary, thyme and salt and pepper.

Melt the remaining oil and butter in the casserole dish and lightly sauté the apple slices. Return the pheasants to the dish.

In a jug mix together well the cider, double cream and cinnamon and pour the mixture over the pheasants. Cover the casserole and cook in the oven at 350°F-180°C-Gas Mark 4 for 50-60 minutes or until the pheasants are cooked. Season to taste.

Place the pheasants on a warmed serving dish and arrange the apples around them. Pour the sauce over the birds and sprinkle with chopped parsley.

~

PORK

Carota Pork

6 thick slices of boneless belly
  pork
2 oz (50 g) butter
2 onions, sliced
1 clove garlic, crushed
8 oz (225 g) carrots, sliced
1 teaspoon mild curry powder
3 teaspoons soy sauce
4 tablespoons chicken stock
pepper
8 oz (225 g) white cabbage,
  shredded
4 oz (110 g) peas, fresh or
  frozen

A GOOD EXAMPLE OF HOW THE SIMPLE INGREDIENTS HERE – CAB-
BAGE, CARROTS, PEAS AND BELLY PORK – CAN BE TRANSFORMED WITH
A FEW EASILY AVAILABLE FLAVOURINGS, GARLIC, SOY SAUCE AND
CURRY POWDER. IT'S VERY TASTY.

Remove the rind from the pork slices and cut each slice in half.

Heat the butter in a saucepan and gently fry the pork slices for 5
minutes, turning once. Add the onions, garlic and carrots and
continue to fry gently for 5 minutes more, giving the mixture an
occasional stir. Then add the curry powder, mixing in well, the
soy sauce, chicken stock and a little pepper.

Cover the pan and simmer gently for about 20 minutes until the
pork is tender.

In another pan cook the cabbage with the peas by steaming for
about 3 minutes until tender crisp.

Stir the vegetables into the cooked pork mixture.

Check the seasoning and serve at once.

~

Chilli Sausage Casserole

1 lb (450 g) best quality pork
  sausagemeat
1 teaspoon rosemary, chopped
1 teaspoon sage, chopped
1 teaspoon thyme, chopped
1 teaspoon paprika
1 tablespoon oil
1 lb (450 g) green cabbage,
  shredded
1 large onion, sliced
15 oz (425 g) can red kidney
  beans
1 tablespoon chilli seasoning
1 level tablespoon flour
1 clove garlic, crushed
¼ pint (150 ml) red wine
¾ pint (425 ml) stock
1 tablespoon tomato purée
1 tablespoon soft dark brown
  sugar
salt and freshly ground black
  pepper

THIS IS TRULY A BIG-HEARTED DISH, PRESENTING AT FIRST GLANCE A
LENGTHY LIST OF INGREDIENTS. BUT THERE'S NOTHING DIFFICULT
ABOUT IT AND IT'S SURE TO GET A GOOD RECEPTION.

Place the sausagemeat in a bowl and work in the three herbs and
the paprika. With well floured hands roll the sausagemeat into 16
balls – about the size of golf balls.

Heat the oil in a frying pan and fry the sausage balls until lightly
browned. Remove with a slotted spoon to a plate. Retain the pan
and its juices.

Take a shallow 3 pint (1.75 litre) casserole dish and place in
layers the cabbage, the onion, the kidney beans and the sausage.

In the pan you used to fry the sausagemeat, add the chilli seasoning, flour and garlic, and stir round, mixing well with the pan
residue (adding a spot more oil if necessary) and cook for 1
minute. Stir in the wine, stock, tomato purée, sugar and seasoning and bring to the boil.

Pour over the ingredients in the casserole dish, cover tightly
and bake in the oven at 350°F-180°C-Gas Mark 4 for about 1 hour.

Hanover Hotpot

*1 lb (450g) smoked back bacon
  in one piece*
1 lb (450g) potatoes
8 oz (225g) carrots
2 tablespoons oil
1 pint (570 ml) chicken stock
bouquet garni
*2 teaspoons fresh dill weed,
  chopped*
pepper
8 oz (225g) runner beans, sliced
8 oz (225g) broad beans
*1 large cooking apple, peeled
  and sliced*
2 teaspoons cornflour
1 tablespoon water

MAKE THE MOST OF FRESH RUNNER AND BROAD BEANS WHEN
THEY'RE IN SEASON AND WITH THE BACON THEY RESULT IN A LOVELY
MEAL.

De-rind the bacon and cut into pieces. Peel and dice the potatoes
and carrots.

In a large saucepan heat the oil and gently fry the bacon,
potatoes and carrots until they change colour. Then stir in the
stock, bouquet garni, 1 teaspoon of dill and pepper to taste. Bring
to the boil, cover and simmer for 15 minutes.

Stir in the beans and the sliced apple.

In the small bowl mix the cornflour with the water and stir into
the pan. Cover again and cook for a further 15 minutes. Remove
the bouquet garni and serve garnished with chopped dill weed.

~

Madeira Pork

6 thin slices pork fillet
1 tablespoon flour
1 teaspoon sage, chopped
1 tablespoon oil
2 tablespoons butter
3 tablespoons chicken stock
*1 dessertspoon onion, finely
  chopped*
*1 dessertspoon bacon, finely
  chopped*
1 dessertspoon parsley, chopped
½ glass Madeira
salt and pepper

IF WINE MERCHANTS' SHELVES ARE ANY GUIDE THEN MADEIRA WINE
SEEMS TO BE MAKING A COMEBACK AND A VERY PLEASANT DRINK IT IS
TOO. THE FRENCH HAVE ALWAYS APPRECIATED ITS VALUE IN THE
KITCHEN, AS THIS VERY ENJOYABLE RECIPE DEMONSTRATES.

Dip the pork slices into the flour, seasoned with the sage. Heat the
oil and butter together in a pan until the butter begins to foam.
Quickly brown the pork on both sides and remove to a warm
plate.

Add to the juices in the pan the stock, onion, bacon, parsley
and Madeira. Stir everything around over a medium heat and
when the sauce begins to turn syrupy return the pork slices.

Heat through for 30 seconds, turning once or twice. Add seasoning to taste and serve immediately.

~

Peppery Pork

4 prime pork chops
salt and freshly ground black
* pepper*
1 tablespoon French mustard
2 tablespoons olive oil
juice and zest of 1 lemon
2 tablespoons demerara sugar
1 tablespoon curry powder
1 clove garlic, crushed

to garnish
1 red pepper
gherkin or cucumber

WITH VERY LITTLE TROUBLE THESE CHOPS ACHIEVE GREAT TASTE AND GOOD LOOKS TO MATCH.

Place the chops in a buttered ovenproof dish. Season them with salt and pepper.

In a bowl mix together the mustard, oil, lemon juice and zest, sugar, curry powder and garlic. Stir together very thoroughly and then pour over the pork.

Place in the oven at 400°F-200°C-Gas Mark 6 and cook for 45-50 minutes.

Prepare the red pepper by removing the core and seeds and cutting the flesh into dice. Peel and dice the gherkin or cucumber.

When cooked place the pork on to a serving dish with the juices and sprinkle the red pepper and gherkin dice over the top.

~

Pork Chops with Mustard Sauce

4 pork loin chops, about 1" (2.5
* cm) thick*
1 tablespoon oil
3 tablespoons butter
salt and pepper
1 egg yolk
1 tablespoon Dijon mustard
3 tablespoons double cream
1 glass dry white wine
2 tablespoons water
1 clove garlic, crushed
2 teaspoons tarragon, chopped
1 teaspoon brandy

THE ALMOST MAGICAL MIXTURE OF TARRAGON, MUSTARD AND CREAM GIVES THE MOST MOUTHWATERING MEAL.

Dry the chops by patting with kitchen paper.

In a heavy pan heat the oil with the butter, until the butter begins to foam, and then add the pork chops and brown well on both sides. Sprinkle the chops with salt and pepper. Cover, reduce the heat, and simmer for 15 minutes.

While the chops are cooking, prepare the sauce flavourings. In a small bowl beat together the egg yolk and mustard. Stir in the cream, and put to one side.

Remove the chops to a warm serving dish.

Turn up the heat under the pan and pour in the wine and water, scraping all the juices from the bottom. Add the garlic, tarragon and salt and pepper. Boil for 1 minute.

Remove the pan from the heat and add the mustard-cream. Stir well and then return to a gentle heat, stirring until the sauce thickens. Do not allow it to boil. Add the brandy, and salt and pepper to taste, then spoon the sauce liberally over the cooked pork chops.

Pork Pizzaiola

SERVES 2

8 oz (225 g) pork fillet
2 tablespoons oil
1 clove garlic
1 oz (25 g) plain flour
salt and black pepper
4 tablespoons dry white wine
2 teaspoons tomato purée
4 tablespoons boiling water
1 oz (25 g) butter
pinch of oregano, chopped
heaped teaspoon capers, lightly
  crushed
chopped parsley to garnish

TWO SIMPLE COOKING STAGES ARE ALL THAT'S NEEDED TO TURN OUT THIS ITALIAN-INSPIRED MASTERPIECE.

Cut the pork fillet into thin discs and place between two layers of cling film or greaseproof paper. Beat out lightly.

Heat the oil and gently fry the whole garlic clove until brown, then remove from the pan and discard.

Dust the pork slices with a light coating of flour and in the same pan quickly fry them on both sides until slightly browned. Remove to a warm plate and season with salt and pepper.

Spoon most of the oil out of the pan and then pour in the wine. Mix the tomato purée with the boiling water and add to the pan, stirring well. Add the butter, and continue cooking, stirring to blend everything together until the mixture thickens slightly. Add the oregano and capers and cook for a minute or so and then return the pork to the pan to heat through, turning a couple of times in the sauce.

Serve at once with a light sprinkling of chopped parsley.

～

Pork Slice with Rice

SERVES 4

2 lb (900 g) belly pork
oil
2 onions, finely chopped
salt and pepper
6 tablespoons dry white wine or
    cider
4 tablespoons soy sauce
2 teaspoons mustard powder
2 teaspoons powdered ginger
2 tablespoons soft brown sugar

for the rice
8 oz (225 g) long-grain rice
2 tablespoons sunflower seeds
2 dessertspoons sesame seeds
1 red pepper

ALTHOUGH IT WOULDN'T BE WISE TO EAT BELLY PORK EVERY DAY IT OFFERS GREAT VALUE, AND THIS HANDSOME DISH CERTAINLY MAKES THE MOST OF IT.

Preheat the oven to 400°F-200°C-Gas Mark 6.

Cut the pork into slices and brush each slice with a little oil. Then lay them in an ovenproof dish, scatter over the onion and some salt and pepper. Bake in the oven for 20 minutes.

In a bowl mix together the wine or cider, soy sauce, mustard powder, ginger and brown sugar.

When the 20 minutes cooking time is up, pour this mixture over the pork slices and continue baking for a further 25-30 minutes, basting the meat a couple of times during cooking.

Meanwhile cook the rice in plenty of boiling salted water for 12 minutes.

Put the sunflower and sesame seeds into a small dry pan over a moderate heat and gently toast them for a few minutes. Drain the rice and run under the cold tap in strainer. Rest the strainer of rice over a pan containing 1" (2.5 cm) of boiling water. Cover the rice with a folded clean tea-towel (taking care that it does not hang over the heat), and steam the rice for 1-2 minutes.

Turn the rice into a bowl. Stir in the toasted seeds. De-seed and chop the red pepper into fine dice. Add these with a dash of soy sauce to the rice. Mix everything well.

Serve the pork with the rice.

~

Pork with Parsnips

1½ lb (700 g) lean pork
2 tablespoons oil
1 tablespoon coriander seeds,
    coarsely crushed
1 large onion, chopped
salt and pepper
3 tablespoons plain flour
2 dessertspoons Dijon mustard
¾ pint (425 ml) chicken stock
1 bay leaf
1 lb (450 g) parsnips, peeled
    and cubed
2 tablespoons chopped parsley

SEASONAL THOUGH THEY MAY BE, WHEN PARSNIPS ARE PLENTIFUL DON'T MISS OUT ON THE OPPORTUNITY TO TRY THIS DELICIOUS DISH.

Trim the pork of any fat and cut into cubes.

Heat the oil and brown the pork, scattering over the coriander seeds during the cooking. Add the onion and cook gently for 3-4 minutes. Season with salt and pepper and then stir in the flour. Mix well and then add the mustard, pour on the stock and add the bay leaf. Bring to the boil and allow to simmer gently for 15 minutes. Then add the cubed parsnips and continue to simmer for 30 minutes or until everything is tender.

Stir in the chopped parsley just before serving.

~

Rooftop Casserole

1½ lb (700 g) pork sparerib
1 oz (25 g) flour
1 oz (25 g) butter
2 medium onions, sliced
2 cooking apples
½ pint (275 ml) dry cider
2 teaspoons fresh sage, chopped
salt and pepper
6 large slices bread, ¼" (5 mm)
    thick
2 oz (50 g) butter, melted

THE BUTTERY CRISP TOPPING, WHEN BROKEN, REVEALS THE CLASSIC COMBINATION OF PORK, APPLE, SAGE AND ONION. IT'S INCOMPARABLE.

Preheat the oven to 350°F-180°C-Gas Mark 4.

Cut the pork into cubes and sprinkle with flour.

Melt the butter in a large pan and gently fry the onions until soft. Add the pork and stir-fry until coloured on all sides.

Peel, core and slice the apples and add them to the pan, along with the cider, sage and salt and pepper to taste. Bring to the boil. Transfer to an ovenproof dish or casserole, and cover and cook in the oven for 1 hour.

Meanwhile, remove the crusts from the bread and cut each slice into four strips. After the pork has cooked for 1 hour remove the cover and arrange the bread strips overlapping on top of the pork. Brush carefully with the melted butter and cook in the oven for a further 30 minutes until the 'roof' is crisp and golden.

~

Sausages in White Wine

SERVES 3

1 lb (450 g) herb sausages
1 dessertspoon oil
1 shallot or small onion, minced
5 fl oz (150 ml) dry white wine
juice of 1 lemon
strip of lemon peel
1 teaspoon Dijon mustard
salt and pepper
1 oz (25 g) butter
1 tablespoon flour
watercress to garnish

THE SAUSAGE IS UNDOUBTEDLY ONE OF BRITAIN'S FAVOURITE FOODS AND THEIR QUALITY AND VARIETY HAVE INCREASED GREATLY IN RECENT YEARS. THIS DISH WILL ADD TO THEIR REPUTATION, AND YOURS.

Preheat the oven to 325°F-170°C-Gas Mark 3.

Pierce the sausage skins. Heat the oil in a pan and brown the sausages lightly for about 10 minutes. Remove the sausages and place in a casserole.

Pour off all but 1 tablespoon of the fat from the pan and gently sauté the shallot or onion for about 2 minutes. Add the wine with the lemon juice and peel, the mustard and salt and pepper. Bring to the boil and then pour over the sausages. Cover the casserole with foil and cook in the oven for 1 hour.

In a small frying pan melt the butter, slowly stir in the flour and when it has reached the honeycomb stage, stir in 2 tablespoons of the liquor from the casserole. Let it thicken, stirring, then stir the mixture back into the casserole.

Cook for another 10 minutes, then serve, garnished with watercress.

~

Somerset Stew

SERVES 4

1½ lb (700 g) lean belly pork
1 medium onion
5 whole cloves
8 oz (225 g) dried black-eye or
    haricot beans, soaked
    overnight in cold water
1 tablespoon clear honey
1 pint (570 ml) chicken stock
½ pint (275 ml) apple juice
bouquet garni
3 carrots
2 leeks
2 ribs celery
2 tablespoons Worcestershire
    sauce
1 tablespoon tomato purée
salt and freshly ground black
    pepper

THERE'S PLENTY OF BODY AND NOURISHMENT ON OFFER FOR THE FAMILY WITH THIS STEW, AND CLOVES AND HONEY TO ADD EXTRA INTEREST.

Rind, bone and cut the pork into chunks. Skin the onion, but leave whole and stick the cloves into the onion at regular intervals around it.

Cook the pork in a flameproof casserole dish over a high heat until the fat runs. Place the onion stuck with the cloves into the dish with the pork.

Drain the beans and add them to the casserole dish along with the honey, stock, apple juice and bouquet garni. Slowly bring to the boil, boil rapidly for 10 minutes, then cover and simmer gently for 1 hour or until the beans are just becoming tender.

Meanwhile prepare the vegetables. Peel and slice the carrots. Wash the leeks thoroughly, trim and slice, and wipe the celery before slicing.

When the pork has cooked for an hour add the carrots, leeks and celery to the casserole with the Worcestershire sauce and tomato purée.

Season to taste and then continue simmering for a further 15-30 minutes or until the beans are really tender.

Discard the bouquet garni before serving. Accompany with crusty bread.

~

Spaghetti alla Carbonara

SERVES 4

1 lb (450 g) spaghetti
salt
8 oz (225 g) streaky bacon, de-
    rinded
3 eggs
4 tablespoons double cream
2 tablespoons chopped parsley
2 oz (50 g) Parmesan cheese,
    grated
freshly ground black pepper
2 oz (50 g) butter

'CHARCOAL BURNERS' STYLE' IS THE MEANING OF THE TITLE – AND ITS SIMPLE, LOVELY STYLE IS WHAT THIS DISH IS ALL ABOUT.

Cook the spaghetti in plenty of boiling salted water until al dente – about 12 minutes. Drain well.

Meanwhile fry the bacon in its own fat until crisp. Drain well and chop.

In a bowl beat the eggs with the cream, parsley, cheese, salt and plenty of pepper.

Melt the butter in a large saucepan, add the egg mixture and stir until just beginning to thicken. Add the cooked spaghetti and the bacon and mix well. Serve immediately.

Spicy Pork

SERVES 4

2 lb (900 g) pork fillet
2 cloves garlic, crushed
½" (1 cm) root ginger, crushed
or 2 pieces preserved ginger,
thinly sliced
1 teaspoon rosemary, chopped
1 teaspoon allspice
1 tablespoon clear honey
1 tablespoon tomato purée
5 fl oz (150 ml) dry sherry
juice of 1 lemon
1 tablespoon vegetable oil
peel of 1 orange, in large pieces
salt and pepper
8 oz (225 g) mushrooms, sliced

to garnish
orange slices
chopped parsley

THE MARINADE HERE INCLUDES GINGER, ORANGE PEEL AND ALL-SPICE AS JUST THREE OF THE INGREDIENTS THAT WILL KEEP YOUR GUESTS GUESSING AS THEY ENJOY THIS GLAMOROUS DINNER PARTY DISH.

Slice the pork fillet into discs.

In a large bowl place all the ingredients except the mushrooms. Stir gently together and leave in the refrigerator overnight or for at least 5 hours. Turn the ingredients occasionally during that time, if possible.

When ready to cook, remove the orange peel and put the rest of the ingredients into a pan with the sliced mushrooms, bring slowly to the boil, cover and then simmer for about 30 minutes, giving an occasional stir. If necessary, a little stock or sherry may be added.

Place on a serving dish surrounded by fresh orange slices and sprinkled with chopped parsley.

~

TURKEY

Turkey Fillets with Mushrooms

THE DELICATE RICHNESS OF THE CREAM AND EGG YOLK THICKENED SAUCE COMPLEMENTS PERFECTLY EVERY TENDER MOUTHFUL OF TURKEY BREAST. A REAL TREAT.

SERVES 2

2 × 6 oz (175 g) turkey fillets
seasoned flour
2 oz (50 g) butter
1 teaspoon oil
1 clove garlic, crushed
2 oz (50 g) mushrooms,
    chopped
1 tablespoon parsley, chopped
3 oz (75 g) Swiss cheese, grated
1 oz (25 g) butter
1 oz (25 g) plain flour
7 fl oz (200 ml) chicken stock
3 fl oz (75 ml) cream
1 egg yolk
salt and pepper

Lightly dust the turkey fillets with seasoned flour. Heat the oil and 2 oz (50 g) butter together and cook the turkey until the juices run clear. Remove from the pan and keep warm.

Add to the pan the garlic, chopped mushrooms, parsley and grated cheese and cook together gently for 5-6 minutes. Keep warm.

In another pan melt the 1 oz (25 g) of butter and stir in the flour. When blended, slowly add the chicken stock, stirring all the time until the mixture thickens. Allow to cook for 3-4 minutes. Remove the pan from the heat.

Mix together the cream and the egg yolk with 2 tablespoons of the thickened hot stock and stir this into the pan. Then add the mushroom mixture to the sauce and stir well. Season to taste and heat everything gently together. Place the turkey fillets on a warm serving dish and spoon the sauce over them.

~

Turkey Pilaff

WHILST THIS DISH FOLLOWS THE POPULAR MIDDLE EASTERN METHOD OF RICE BASED DISHES, THE ABSENCE OF ANY EXOTIC SPICES OR FLAVOURINGS MAKES IT SUITABLE FOR PALATES OF ALL AGES.

SERVES 4

12 oz (350 g) turkey fillets
2 tablespoons oil
1 oz (25 g) butter
1 onion, finely sliced
2 carrots, diced
12 oz (350 g) rice, long-grain or
    risotto rice
4 oz (110 g) peas
1 tablespoon mild mustard
1½ pints (850 ml) chicken stock
salt and pepper
dash of Worcestershire sauce

Remove any skin from the turkey and cut into bite-sized pieces. Heat the oil and butter in a pan and stir in the chopped onion and fry gently until soft. Add the diced carrots and continue cooking. Add the rice, turning it in the pan to coat it with the oil. Then add the turkey and peas. Stir in the mustard and gradually add about 1 pint (570 ml) of the stock. Season with a little salt and pepper and the Worcestershire sauce.

Cover the pan and simmer gently for 20 minutes, checking to see that the mixture does not become too dry. Add a little more stock if necessary.

Tip the pilaff on to a hot serving dish. Fluff up with a fork and serve.

Turkey Treat

SERVES 4

12 oz (350 g) turkey breast,
   minced
2 oz (50 g) fresh white
   breadcrumbs
4 spring onions, finely chopped
grated zest of 1 lemon
8 cardamom pods, seeds
   removed and crushed
1 egg, beaten
½ teaspoon chilli powder
salt
1 tablespoon oil
1 oz (25 g) butter

THE BLANDNESS OF THE MINCED TURKEY PROVIDES A BRILLIANT BACKGROUND FOR THE CARDAMOM, LEMON AND CHILLI HIGHLIGHTS.

In a bowl mix the minced turkey with the breadcrumbs, chopped onions, lemon zest, crushed cardamom seeds, beaten egg, chilli powder and salt. Mix everything very well together and then form the mixture into balls (with wetted hands to prevent sticking).

Heat the oil and butter in a pan and gently fry the turkey balls, turning occasionally until cooked through.

Serve with a homemade tomato sauce and salad.

~

TEATIME SNACKS

Janssen's Temptation

SERVES 4

12 oz (350 g) potatoes, thinly sliced
8 oz (225 g) onion, thinly sliced
2 oz (50 g) can anchovy fillets, finely chopped
3 oz (75 g) butter
1½ oz (40 g) fresh white breadcrumbs
6 fl oz (175 ml) single cream
2 oz (50 g) Cheddar cheese, finely grated

SWEDEN HAS GIVEN THE WORLD THIS MARVELLOUS POTATO DISH OF WHICH THERE ARE MANY VARIATIONS. THIS ONE HAS A CHEDDAR TOPPING FOR EXTRA GOOD LOOKS.

Preheat the oven to 400°F-200°C-Gas Mark 6.

Mix the potatoes with the onions, finely chopped anchovies and their oil. Thickly butter an ovenproof dish with 1½ oz (40 g) butter. Turn the potato mixture into the buttered dish.

Melt the remaining butter slowly and turn the breadcrumbs in it so they are well coated. Sprinkle them over the potatoes. Cover the dish with foil and bake in the oven for 35 minutes.

Remove the foil and pour the cream in at one side. Sprinkle with the grated cheese and return to the oven uncovered and bake for a further 20-30 minutes until the potatoes are cooked and the crumbs golden brown.

~

Mushroom Pasta

SERVES 4

12 oz (350 g) button mushrooms
2 tablespoons oil
1 large onion, finely chopped
1 clove garlic, crushed
2 rashers bacon, chopped
14 oz (396 g) can tomatoes
2 fl oz (55 ml) chicken stock
salt and pepper
½ teaspoon oregano
1 lb (450 g) spaghetti
grated Parmesan cheese (optional)

I'M SORRY TO SAY THAT I FIND THE MAJORITY OF BOTTLED PASTA SAUCES RATHER LACKING, WHICH IS WHY, FOR EXAMPLE, THIS SAUCE AMPLY REWARDS THE EFFORT INVOLVED.

Wipe the mushrooms and remove their stalks. Heat the oil in a saucepan. Add the onion, garlic and bacon and fry until soft but not brown. Add the mushrooms and cook, stirring occasionally for 5 minutes, over a very low heat.

Drain and chop the tomatoes and add to the pan with the chicken stock. Season with salt, pepper and oregano. Lower the heat and simmer gently for 15 minutes, stirring occasionally.

Meanwhile cook the spaghetti in plenty of boiling salted water for about 12 minutes until just tender, then drain well.

Put the spaghetti in a deep serving dish, pour over the sauce and sprinkle with grated Parmesan cheese, if wished.

~

Mustard and Walnut Scone Ring

SERVES 4

8 oz (225g) self-raising flour
pinch of salt
2 oz (50 g) butter
3 oz (75 g) Cheddar cheese,
  grated
1 egg, beaten
6 tablespoons milk (approx)
2 teaspoons made English
  mustard
1 oz (25 g) walnuts

A DELICIOUS SAVOURY SCONE WITH A GENTLE MUSTARD AND CHEDDAR TANG.

Preheat the oven to 425°F-220°C-Gas Mark 7.

Sieve the flour and salt into a mixing bowl. Add the butter cut into small pieces and rub in until the mixture resembles fine crumbs. Stir in 2 oz (50 g) of the grated cheese, followed by the beaten egg and sufficient milk to mix to a soft dough.

Knead lightly on a floured surface then roll out to an oblong about 10″ × 8″ (25.5 × 20 cm). Spread the mustard all over the pastry and then sprinkle the walnuts over the top. Roll up the dough, starting with one of the long sides and press the join to seal it. Cut the roll into 10 equal slices and lay them flat, in a circle on a greased baking sheet.

Sprinkle with the remaining 1 oz (25 g) of cheese and bake in the oven for 20 minutes.

Best eaten on the day of baking.

~

Onion Tart

SERVES 4

for the pastry
7 oz (200 g) plain flour
2 oz (50 g) butter
1½ oz (40 g) lard
cold water to mix

for the filling
1½ lb (700 g) large onions
1½ oz (40 g) butter
3 eggs
8 fl oz (225 ml) milk
salt and pepper
pinch of nutmeg

WHERE WOULD WE COOKS BE WITHOUT THE ONION? IN A BAD WAY I THINK. HERE'S A FINE FAMILY TART TO CELEBRATE ITS VIRTUES.

First make the pastry. Sift the flour into a large bowl and add the butter and lard cut into pieces. Rub in the fats until the mixture resembles breadcrumbs. Add enough cold water to mix to a firm dough. Turn on to a floured surface and roll out to fit an 8″ (20 cm) flan tin. Prick the base of the pastry all over with a fork and set aside in the fridge while you make the filling.

Slice the onions very thinly in rings. Melt 1½ oz (40 g) butter in a heavy pan and add the onions, cover and cook very slowly until they start to soften.

In a bowl beat the eggs with the milk and add salt and pepper and nutmeg to taste.

When the onions are beginning to soften, lift them out with a slotted spoon and add them to the egg and milk mixture. Pour this into the pastry case and bake in the oven at 425°F-220°C-Gas Mark 7 for 35-40 minutes until the pastry is cooked and the filling set, with a golden brown top. Delicious either hot or cold.

Patates Catalana

SERVES 4

2 large baking potatoes
1 red pepper
2 hard-boiled eggs, shelled
4 anchovy fillets
2 oz (50 g) butter
3 tablespoons minced shallots or
    spring onions
1 tablespoon chives, chopped
3 tablespoons soured cream
salt and pepper
2 oz (50 g) butter, melted
chopped parsley to garnish

I FIRST HEARD OF THIS RECIPE IN BARCELONA AND QUITE BY CHANCE CAME ACROSS IT AGAIN LAST YEAR. THE COMBINATION OF FLAVOURS REALLY TRANSFORMS THE HUMBLE BAKED POTATO. IF YOU'VE NEVER SKIN ROASTED A RED PEPPER BEFORE, DON'T WORRY: IT'S QUITE SIMPLE.

Scrub the potatoes and dry them. Bake in the oven at 400°F-200°C-Gas Mark 6 for about 1 hour or until done.

Grill the red pepper until the skin is completely black on all sides. Holding the pepper on the end of a fork, carefully place under cold running water and gently rub the skin, which will peel off quite effortlessly. Cut the flesh into strips and de-seed.

Chop the hard-boiled eggs. Coarsely chop the anchovies.

When they are cooked, cut the potatoes in half and carefully scoop out the insides with a spoon. Set the scooped-out portion aside and return the potato skins to the oven for about 5 minutes or until slightly crisp. Melt 2 oz (50 g) butter in a pan and sauté the shallot or onion until soft. Mash the potatoes and then stir in the sautéd shallots.

In another bowl mix together the anchovies, eggs and strips of pepper. Stir in the chopped chives and then add the mixture to the mashed potatoes. Stir in the soured cream, salt and pepper to taste and mix everything well together.

Place the potato skins in an ovenproof gratin dish and refill them with the potato mixture, drizzle melted butter over each one and then return them to the oven for about 20 minutes or until they are golden brown.

Garnish with chopped parsley.

~

Plain Scones

MAKES 8

8 oz (225 g) self-raising flour
½ teaspoon salt
2 oz (50 g) lard
milk to make a soft dough

PROBABLY THE BEST TEA-TIME TREAT EVER.

Mix the flour and salt together in a bowl. Rub in the lard and add enough milk to form a soft dough. Knead lightly on a floured board and roll out to just over ½" (1 cm) in thickness.

Cut in rounds 2½" (6.5 cm) and re-roll the trimmings to cut more rounds. Place on a greased baking tray. If you like a golden finish to your scones then brush the tops with egg and milk.

Bake in the oven at 425°F-220°C-Gas Mark 7 for about 10 minutes.

~

Spicy Bean Goulash

SERVES 4

6 oz (175 g) aduki beans, soaked
overnight or 14 oz (400 g)
can red kidney beans, drained
and rinsed
1 tablespoon oil
8 oz (225 g) onion, finely
chopped
1 clove garlic, crushed
1 small red chilli, finely chopped
2 courgettes, diced
1 large red pepper, de-seeded
and diced
8 oz (225 g) mushrooms, wiped
and chopped
1 medium potato, peeled and
diced
3 teaspoons paprika
1 teaspoon thyme
2 tablespoons tomato purée
1 teaspoon yeast extract
salt and black pepper

THE TERM GOULASH COMES FROM THE HUNGARIAN WORD *GULYAS*, MEANING HERDSMAN. WHENEVER I'VE AIRED THAT PIECE OF KNOW-LEDGE AT THE DINNER TABLE THE REACTION HAS BEEN RATHER NEGATIVE, SO YOU MIGHT BE WELL ADVISED TO KEEP IT TO YOURSELF. THIS RECIPE ON THE OTHER HAND IS WELL WORTH PASSING AROUND.

Drain the aduki beans after soaking overnight. Place in a sauce-pan and cover with fresh water. Bring to a fast boil for 10 minutes, then reduce the heat and simmer for 40 minutes. Drain and re-serve the stock. Heat the oil in a pan and fry the onions with the garlic for 3 minutes. Then add the chilli, courgettes, red pepper and the mushrooms. Cook in the pan, covered, for 15-20 minutes over a very gentle heat.

After that time, add the cooked aduki beans, or the drained red kidney beans, and the diced potato, paprika, thyme, tomato purée and yeast extract. Simmer gently for 30 minutes, adding a little bean stock, or water, if necessary.

Season well, and serve hot with brown rice or wholewheat noodles.

~

Wonder Omelette

6 oz (175 g) potatoes
4 oz (110 g) French beans
4 oz (110 g) ham or any
  Continental sausage
½ red pepper
2 oz (50 g) mushrooms
1 medium onion
2 oz (50 g) butter
1 tablespoon oil
1 clove garlic, crushed
4 eggs, beaten
2 oz (50 g) Parmesan cheese,
  grated

ANOTHER VERSION OF THE SPANISH OMELETTE FOR WHICH THE GAR-
LIC AND PARMESAN CHEESE DO WONDERS.

Peel and boil the potatoes and when cooked cut into dice. Cook
the French beans and cut up. Dice the ham or sausage. De-seed
and dice the red pepper. Slice the mushrooms. Peel and chop the
onion.

Melt the butter and oil in a large omelette pan and cook the
onion gently until soft. Then add to the pan the crushed clove of
garlic, the potatoes, French beans, ham or sausage, red pepper
and mushrooms and warm everything through.

Beat the eggs and add them to the pan, shaking the pan gently
to distribute the egg evenly.

Sprinkle on the grated Parmesan cheese, cover the pan and
allow to cook very gently for about 10 minutes until the egg is set.
Before serving flash under a hot grill to brown the top.

~

A salad can be anything you want it to be and it can form any part of a meal. Salad makes an excellent first course, being lightweight, attractive in appearance and usually fairly easy to prepare in advance – leaving the addition of the chosen dressing until the last moment.

As an accompaniment (side-salad) it can be a bit of a nuisance, especially since those handy crescent-shaped dishes, designed to follow the contours of the dinner plate, seem to have gone out of fashion, except in some restaurants which use them for vegetables. Even then, to eat correctly, the constant switching of one's fork to the right hand is a tiresome business, so personally I prefer to consume my salad having first disposed of my main dish. There is also the important factor that should you be drinking an exceptional glass of wine, the vinegar-based dressing will interfere with its finer points, which is why, for example, serious wine drinkers will eat a piece of dry bread to clear the palate before tasting a new bottle.

Where the salad is a main dish, cheese, shellfish, bacon, livers and beans are particularly useful for adding protein, weight and interest to a background of the varied leaves, vegetables, fruits and roots. Some of these are of course seasonal although these days we have quite a good all year round choice. The following are a few of my favourites, together with some dressings which can make a world of difference to even the simplest components.

Caesar Salad

SERVES 3 or 6

2 cloves garlic, crushed
8 tablespoons olive oil
4 slices white bread, crusts
    removed
1 iceberg or similar crisp lettuce
2 tablespoons lemon juice
1 teaspoon Worcestershire sauce
freshly ground pepper
8 anchovy fillets, drained and
    cut into thirds
salt
2 hard-boiled egg yolks, sieved
4 tablespoons freshly grated
    Parmesan cheese
chopped parsley to garnish
    (optional)

ONE OF THE BEST SALADS EVER CREATED IN MY OPINION, EXCEPT THAT ONE IS SUPPOSED TO TOSS IN A COUPLE OF RAW, OR ONE-MINUTE BOILED EGGS AT THE MOMENT OF SERVING AND THIS I CANNOT BRING MYSELF TO DO. SO I CHEAT AND SUBSTITUTE SIEVED HARD-BOILED EGG YOLK, WHICH LOOKS A LOT BETTER.

THIS SERVES 3 AS A LIGHT MAIN COURSE OR 6 FIRST COURSES.

Steep the crushed garlic in the olive oil for 30 minutes. Cut the crustless bread into ¼" (5 mm) cubes. Heat half the garlic oil in a pan and fry the bread cubes until they become golden brown croûtons. Remove from pan with a slotted spoon and drain on kitchen paper.

Tear the lettuce leaves into manageable pieces and put into a salad bowl.

Whisk together the remaining oil, lemon juice, Worcestershire sauce, pepper and anchovy pieces. Test taste and if necessary add some salt. Pour this dressing over the lettuce and toss well. Add the croûtons, half of the sieved egg yolk and 3 tablespoons of the grated Parmesan cheese. Toss again to distribute among the leaves and finally sprinkle on top the remaining cheese and sieved egg yolk.

A little freshly chopped parsley, if available, will contrast nicely sprinkled on as well. Serve immediately.

~

Chicken Liver, Walnut and Chicory Salad

SERVES 4

8 oz (225 g) chicken livers
salt
1 oz (25 g) butter
3 heads of chicory (Belgian
    endive)
lettuce leaves
2 oz (50 g) walnut halves
1 tablespoon Sherry vinegar
1 tablespoon walnut oil
1 tablespoon olive oil
freshly ground black pepper
1 teaspoon Dijon mustard
chopped chives to garnish

Slice the chicken livers and season with salt. Melt the butter in a pan and fry the livers gently, until just cooked. Remove and allow to cool.

Arrange the chicory leaves on a plate, place the warm livers in the centre, on a nest of small (or shredded) lettuce leaves. Top the livers with the walnuts.

Mix together the vinegar, the two oils, pepper, salt and Dijon mustard and spoon the dressing over the nuts and livers.

Sprinkle with chopped chives to garnish.

Green Bean Salad

THESE TENDER CRISP FINE GREEN BEANS WITH THEIR HANDSOME WALNUT DRESSING MAKE A LOVELY FIRST COURSE, WITH WARMED FRENCH BREAD ON HAND TO MOP UP THE DELICIOUSLY FLAVOURED OIL.

SERVES 4

1½ lb (700 g) French green
    beans
1 tablespoon white wine vinegar
½ teaspoon Dijon mustard
salt and pepper
1 clove garlic, crushed
3 tablespoons olive oil or
    sunflower oil
2 tablespoons walnuts, chopped
1 tablespoon parsley, chopped

Wash the beans and top and tail them. Cook them in boiling salted water until tender but still quite crisp. Drain and immediately refresh them under cold running water. Place them in a bowl.

In another bowl mix together the vinegar, mustard, salt, pepper and garlic. Then add the oil, beating it in well with a fork. Pour the dressing over the beans, then sprinkle with the walnuts and chopped parsley.

Gently toss the beans to coat them with the dressing and chill for a couple of hours in the fridge before serving.

~

Pasta Shell and Cheese Salad

FOR YEARS I AVOIDED COLD PASTA SALAD CONCOCTIONS BUT THEN I DISCOVERED THIS BRILLIANT IDEA WHICH MAKES A DELICIOUS MEAT-LESS MEAL.

SERVES 4

4 oz (110 g) medium sized pasta
    shells
5 oz (150 g) finely sliced celery
4 oz (110 g) Cheddar cheese,
    grated
4 oz (110 g) cottage cheese
2 oz (50 g) Stilton or Roquefort
    cheese, crumbled
6 spring onions, finely sliced
    including some green part
2 tablespoons finely chopped
    parsley
3 tablespoons olive oil
2 tablespoons lemon juice
1 dessertspoon Dijon mustard
½ teaspoon caster sugar
salt and pepper
salad leaves

Cook the pasta shells according to the packet directions. Rinse with cold water and drain, shaking well.

Place in a large bowl and add the celery, all the cheeses, spring onions and parsley.

In another bowl make a dressing with the oil, lemon juice, mustard and sugar, mixing everything well together. Pour the dressing over the pasta mixture and toss well to coat.

Season to taste with salt and pepper and serve on a nest of salad leaves.

~

Salami Salad

SERVES 4

1 medium head iceberg or cos
   lettuce
2 carrots, peeled
2 tomatoes
4 oz (110 g) sausage
15 oz (425 g) can chick peas,
   drained

for the dressing
3 tablespoons mayonnaise
2 tablespoons soured cream
pinch dry mustard powder
1 small clove garlic, crushed
2-3 dashes of Tabasco sauce
   (more if liked)
salt to taste

ANY CONTINENTAL SAUSAGE YOU FANCY WILL DO HERE, INCLUDING
PEPPERONI WHICH CAN BE BOUGHT PRE-SLICED IN PACKETS AT MOST
SUPERMARKETS.

Wash the lettuce dry and then tear into pieces. Peel the carrots
and cut into fine 2″ (5 cm) sticks. Skin, de-seed and chop the tomatoes. If you have chosen a small sausage then slice it, if a large
sausage then cut into dice. In a large bowl combine all the salad ingredients, mixing them together well.

In another bowl make the dressing by mixing together the
mayonnaise, soured cream, mustard powder, garlic, Tabasco and
salt. Blend everything together and then toss with a spoon and
fork to coat. Serve immediately.

~

Watercress and Chicken Liver Salad

SERVES 1

½ bunch watercress
1 oz (25 g) butter
2 teaspoons oil
3 oz (75 g) chicken livers,
   halved
1 tablespoon French dressing

A DELICIOUS SAVOURY SALAD WHICH CAN BE SERVED AS A FIRST
COURSE OR LIGHT LUNCH DISH.

Allow half a bunch of trimmed watercress per person and arrange
on a medium sized plate.

Heat the butter and oil together and quickly fry the halved
chicken livers. Avoid overcooking – they should still be a little
pink inside.

Lift livers out with a slotted spoon and scatter over the watercress. Then add to the pan residues the tablespoon of French
dressing. As soon as it bubbles up, which it will very quickly,
spoon this hot dressing over the livers and watercress and serve
immediately.

~

French Apple Tart (page 141) and
Lemon Meringue Pie (page 143).

Dundee Cake (page 129), *Mustard and Walnut Scone Ring*
(page 107) and *Chocolate Chip Cookies* (page 120).

Classic French Dressing (Vinaigrette)

1 level teaspoon Dijon mustard
½ teaspoon salt
½ teaspoon pepper
5 fl oz (150 ml) white wine
vinegar
12 fl oz (330 ml) olive or
sunflower oil

THE BEST WAY TO MAKE THIS IS BY THE ½ LITRE (17 FL OZ) – AND AN EMPTY OIL BOTTLE MAKES THE IDEAL CONTAINER. WITH THE BACK OF A KNIFE CAREFULLY PRISE OFF THE HANDY PLASTIC POURER, AND PROCEED TO MAKE THE DRESSING.

Use your little finger to scrape the mustard into the bottle, followed by the salt and pepper. Now pour in the white wine vinegar, replace the screw cap and give the bottle a good shaking, to break down the mustard. Now fill the bottle with your chosen oil – an equal mixture of olive and sunflower will suit most palates – replace the plastic pourer and the screw cap and shake again, until the contents are well blended, and that's it.

Between use, of course, the contents will separate, making it necessary to give another few shakes before pouring.

To give a change of accent to the basic dressing, add any of the following groups of ingredients to 5 fl oz (150 ml) of dressing.

VARIATION 1
1 tablespoon chopped parsley
1 tablespoon chopped chives or spring onion
1 finely grated hard-boiled egg

VARIATION 2
1 oz (25 g) finely crumbled blue cheese
1 dessertspoon finely chopped shallot

VARIATION 3
(very good with bean sprouts and Chinese leaves)
2 tablespoons light soy sauce
2 tablespoons toasted sesame seeds

~

Balsamic Vinegar

A FEW YEARS AGO A FRIEND KINDLY BROUGHT ME FROM ITALY A BOTTLE OF THIS UNIQUE PRODUCT, WHICH HAPPILY IS NOW WIDELY AVAILABLE. DARK IN COLOUR, IT IS PREPARED ACCORDING TO A CENTURIES-OLD TRADITION IN MODENA, AND EVER SINCE THAT FIRST BOTTLE I HAVE USED NOTHING ELSE WHEN MAKING FRENCH AND OTHER DRESSINGS. ITS DIFFERENCE FROM MORE USUAL VINEGARS IS REMARKABLE AND I SINCERELY URGE YOU TO GIVE IT A TRY. ITS RICH SWEETLY DISTINCTIVE FLAVOUR IS HIGHLY ADDICTIVE.

Mayonnaise

I DON'T OFTEN TROUBLE TO MAKE THIS AND NOR, I SUSPECT, DO MOST PEOPLE, PARTICULARLY WHERE EVERYDAY COOKING AND EATING ARE CONCERNED. THERE ARE A FEW VERY ACCEPTABLE COMMERCIAL BRANDS AVAILABLE – THE ONLY DRAWBACK BEING THAT THEY CAN SOMETIMES BE A LITTLE TOO THICK FOR POURING AND COATING PURPOSES. THE SIMPLE REMEDY THERE IS QUICKLY TO STIR IN A TABLESPOON OR SO OF BOILING WATER UNTIL THE DESIRED CONSISTENCY IS ACHIEVED.

~

Yoghurt Dressing

To make 5 fl oz (150 ml)

5 fl oz (150 ml) natural yoghurt
1 tablespoon vegetable oil
1 teaspoon cider vinegar
1 teaspoon runny honey
½ teaspoon Dijon mustard

THIS DRESSING HAS GREAT APPEAL AS AN ALTERNATIVE TO MAYONNAISE FOR THE CALORIE CONSCIOUS AND THE 'GREEK-STYLE' NATURAL YOGHURT SEEMS NICER TO ME THAN ANY OTHER.

Simply mix the ingredients well together and if time allows chill before serving.

~

Egg and Herb Sauce

Serves 4, generously

4 hard-boiled eggs
1 tablespoon chopped parsley
1 tablespoon English mustard
1 tablespoon white wine vinegar
salt and black pepper
8 fl oz (225 ml) oil

optional additions
tarragon, chives, capers,
*   shallots, chilli peppers*

A CLASSIC SAUCE IN ITS OWN RIGHT AND AN IDEAL SUBSTITUTE FOR MAYONNAISE IF YOU WISH TO AVOID USING RAW EGG YOLKS.

Shell the hard-boiled eggs and separate the yolks from the whites. Chop the egg whites quite finely and chop the parsley.

Put the egg yolks in a bowl and mash them thoroughly. Then add to them the mustard, wine vinegar, salt and pepper to taste, and mix everything well together. Gradually pour in the oil in a thin stream, beating constantly until the mixture thickens.

Then add the chopped parsley together with the chopped egg whites and any combination of the following ingredients: fresh tarragon, chives, capers, finely chopped shallot or even a small hot chilli pepper.

~

Fresh Tomato Sauce

SERVES 6

1 large onion, sliced
2 carrots, coarsely chopped
1 stick celery, coarsely chopped
2 lb (900 g) tomatoes, skinned
  and coarsely chopped
6 leaves fresh basil
salt and freshly ground black
  pepper
1 oz (25 g) butter
1 teaspoon sugar (optional)

WITH THE VERY LARGE NUMBER OF COMMERCIAL TOMATO SAUCES ALREADY AVAILABLE EVERYWHERE YOU MAY WELL ASK 'WHY BOTHER?'. PLEASE BELIEVE ME, AS FAR AS THIS RECIPE IS CONCERNED, THERE'S NO COMPARISON.

Put the onion, carrot and celery into a saucepan with the tomatoes. Add the basil and simmer gently for 45 minutes, stirring the sauce occasionally and adding a little water if it becomes too dry. When the vegetables are thoroughly cooked the sauce is done. Add a little salt and pepper.

Pour the sauce into a sieve and allow the liquid to run out. (You can use this for another dish.) Liquidise the remaining sauce in the sieve, and then return it to the pan together with the butter.

Taste, and add a teaspoon of sugar if you feel it is needed.

Return the pan to the heat and bring it barely to the boil, stirring. It is now ready, but will keep very well, covered, in the fridge.

~

Super Sauce

SERVES 2 generously

2 egg yolks
salt and pepper
1 teaspoon Dijon mustard
1 tablespoon chopped fresh herbs
1 tablespoon vinegar
2 oz (50 g) butter

THIS REALLY IS A BRILLIANT SAUCE WHICH TO ME IS FAR MORE INTERESTING THAN PLAIN HOLLANDAISE AND MUCH LESS TROUBLE TO MAKE. TO AVOID CURDLING, THE BUTTER SHOULD BE ONLY JUST MELTED AND THE ADDITION OF A LITTLE FRESHLY CRUSHED GARLIC IS AN EXTRA OPTION.

In a bowl mix everything, except the butter, together. Stir thoroughly.

Melt the butter in a small pan and pour on to the other ingredients. Stir through well and serve at once, while still warm.
A superb sauce for fish, meat, poultry and vegetables.

~

BISCUITS

Brownies

MAKES 24

4 oz (110 g) margarine
2 oz (50 g) plain cooking
  chocolate
6 oz (175 g) soft dark brown
  sugar
2 eggs, beaten
½ teaspoon vanilla essence
2 oz (50 g) self-raising flour
4 oz (110g) chopped walnuts
pinch of salt

THIS MUST BE THE USA'S NUMBER ONE FAVOURITE COOKIE, AND QUITE HONESTLY I'M NOT SURPRISED. THIS RECIPE BELONGS IN THE 'EXTRA GOOD' CLASS.

Melt the margarine and chocolate together in a bowl over a pan of hot water. Remove from the heat and allow to cool. Then stir in the sugar and the eggs. Add the vanilla essence and mix well. Stir in the flour, followed by the chopped nuts and the salt.

Pour the batter into a well greased 11" × 7" (28 cm × 18 cm) tin. Bake in the oven at 350°F-180°C-Gas Mark 4 for 25-30 minutes, until the top is crispy and the inside soft.

Leave to cool in the tin, before cutting into squares.

~

Chocolate Chip Cookies

MAKES 24

3 oz (75 g) margarine
3 oz (75 g) brown sugar
1 egg, beaten
few drops of vanilla essence
pinch of salt
6 oz (175 g) self-raising flour
4 oz (110 g) plain chocolate,
  chopped or 4 oz (110 g)
  chocolate chips

ANOTHER VERY POPULAR BISCUIT. IN FACT THERE'S AN ALMOST CONSTANT QUEUE OF PEOPLE WAITING TO BUY THESE IN SELFRIDGES.

In a bowl cream together the margarine and sugar until light and fluffy. Beat in the egg and vanilla essence. Stir in the sifted flour, salt and chocolate pieces.

Roll the mixture into walnut-sized balls, flatten them and place on a greased baking tray.

Bake in the oven at 350°F-180°C-Gas Mark 4 for about 10-15 minutes.

~

Melting Moments

MAKES 40

2½ oz (60 g) margarine
1½ oz (40 g) lard
3 oz caster sugar
½ egg, beaten
1 teaspoon vanilla essence
5 oz (150 g) self-raising flour
to coat
rolled oats or dessicated coconut
glacé cherries, chopped

IT'S TEN YEARS SINCE I FIRST DISCOVERED THESE IN THE STUDIO CANTEEN AND I'VE BEEN A FAN EVER SINCE.

In a bowl cream the margarine, lard and sugar until very light and fluffy. Beat in the egg and vanilla essence. Stir in the flour and mix well.

Moisten your hands and form the mixture into about 40 small balls.

Have ready the oats or coconut in a dish and toss each ball in your chosen coating.

Place on a greased baking tray, pressing flat lightly, and place a small piece of cherry on each biscuit.

Bake in the oven at 350°F-180°C-Gas Mark 4 for 15-20 minutes.

~

Rich Jumbles

MAKES 18

4 oz (110 g) unsalted butter
4 oz (110 g) caster sugar
1 egg, beaten
1 dessertspoon brandy
6 oz (175 g) plain flour, sifted
flour and caster sugar for
*   rolling out*
icing sugar for dredging

THESE ARE A CENTURIES-OLD FAVOURITE I DISCOVERED WHEN RESEARCHING FOR A FOOD PROGRAMME ABOUT BYGONE DAYS.

In a large bowl cream the butter and sift in the sugar. Then cream them together until light and fluffy. Mix in the egg and the brandy. Gradually mix in the sifted flour, adding an extra 1 oz (25 g) of flour if the dough is too sticky.

Chill it well to firm it up. Roll out on a surface well sprinkled with flour and caster sugar, to a thickness of ¼" (5 mm). Cut into rings with either 2½" or 1½" (4-6 cm) fluted biscuit cutters.

Place on lightly greased baking sheets and cook in the oven at 375°F-190°C-Gas Mark 5 for 8-10 minutes or until a very pale fawn. They should not be brown.

Cool and then store. Dredge with icing sugar before use.

These are delicious alone but also a good accompaniment to ice-cream desserts.

~

Shortbread

MAKES 24

8 oz (225 g) unsalted butter
3 oz (75 g) caster sugar
1 oz (25 g) icing sugar
11 oz (310 g) plain flour
1 oz (25 g) cornflour

JUST THE THING TO ACCOMPANY A CUP OF TEA.

Preheat the oven to 325°F-170°C-Gas Mark 3.

In a bowl cream the butter until very smooth and then gradually work in all the other ingredients. Press the mixture into an 8″ × 12″ (20 × 30 cm) tin, and mark with a fork.

Bake in the preheated oven for 30-35 minutes until pale golden in colour.

Cut into 24 fingers. Leave to cool thoroughly.

Store in an airtight container.

~

CAKES

Apricot and Hazelnut Scones

8 oz (225 g) plain flour
pinch of salt
4 teaspoons baking powder
3 oz (75 g) butter
1 tablespoon granulated sugar
3 oz (75g) no-need-to-soak
 apricots, chopped
3 oz (75 g) hazelnuts, chopped
1 egg, beaten
3 fl oz (75 ml) milk

NO NEED FOR JAM OR CREAM HERE, BUT THEY'RE BEAUTIFUL WITH BUTTER.

Sift the flour, salt and baking powder into a bowl. Rub in the butter until the mixture resembles breadcrumbs. Stir in the sugar, chopped apricots and nuts.

Put the beaten egg into a measuring jug and add enough milk to make up to 5 fl oz (150 ml). Stir this into the flour to make a soft dough.

Knead the dough lightly on a floured board, then roll it out to ½" (1 cm) thickness. Using a 2" (5 cm) cutter, stamp out rounds, re-rolling the trimmings as necessary.

Carefully place the rounds on a greased baking tray and bake until golden brown and well risen.

Cool on a wire rack.

Best served the day they are made.

~

Black Forest Gateau

3 eggs
6 oz (175 g) caster sugar
6 oz (175 g) self-raising flour
2 tablespoons cocoa powder
4 tablespoons hot water

for the filling
½ pint (275 ml) double cream
½ teaspoon vanilla essence
1 dessertspoon caster sugar
14 oz (400 g) can cherry pie
    filling
4 oz (110 g) plain chocolate,
    coarsely grated

FOR YEARS, THIS WAS ONE OF THE MOST POPULAR 'EATING OUT' PUDDINGS. YOU MIGHT LIKE TO SERVE THIS WHEN ENTERTAINING AT HOME, ALTHOUGH MY ADVICE TO THE INEXPERIENCED HAS ALWAYS BEEN, DON'T RISK FIRST-TIME ATTEMPTS WITH GUESTS YOU MAY WANT TO IMPRESS. FAR BETTER TO STAGE A REHEARSAL FOR THE FAMILY. IN THIS PARTICULAR INSTANCE I'M SURE THEY'LL BE DELIGHTED.

Break the eggs into a bowl and whisk lightly. Add the sugar and whisk again until thick and creamy, and very pale in colour.

In a bowl sift the flour and cocoa together and fold into the mixture. Fold in the hot water. Pour the mixture into a greased, and base lined 8″ (20 cm) cake tin.

Bake in the oven at 375°F-190°C-Gas Mark 5 for 35-40 minutes.

Remove from the tin and cool on a wire rack. Cut into three layers.

To make the filling, whip the cream with the vanilla essence and the caster sugar until stiff. Place in a piping bag fitted with a large star nozzle. Pipe one-third of the cream in a border round the bottom layer of the cake.

Remove and reserve 8 cherries from the filling and then spread the remainder in the centre of the bottom layer of the cake. Place the centre cake layer on top. Cover this with half the remaining cream. Cover with the top cake layer. Spread most of the remaining cream on top and round the sides of the cake.

Decorate by pressing the grated chocolate over the cream covered sides of the cake, and in a circle in the centre of the top of the cake. Pipe whirls of cream round the cake top and place a reserved cherry on each one.

~

Brack

8 oz (225 g) sultanas
4 oz (110 g) raisins
4 oz (110 g) currants
6 oz (175 g) demerara sugar
½ pint (150 ml) hot tea
1 egg, beaten
8 oz (225 g) self-raising flour

I USED TO LOVE THIS AS A CHILD AND I STILL DO. IN IRELAND AT HALLOWEEN A GOLD RING IS CONCEALED IN THE MIXTURE TO BE DISCOVERED BY THE LUCKY FINDER.

In a bowl mix together the dried fruit, sugar and hot tea. Cover and leave overnight.

The next day add the beaten egg to the fruit, beat well in and then stir in the flour.

Grease and line a 2 lb (1 kg) loaf tin.

Place the mixture in the tin and bake in the oven at 325°F-170°C-Gas Mark 3 for about 1½-1¾ hours.

Note: It is important to use hot tea for this recipe as it helps the dried fruit to swell.

~

Carrot Cake

1 tablespoon lemon juice
5 fl oz (150 ml) milk
4 oz (110 g) butter
8 fl oz (225 ml) honey
8 oz (225 g) carrots, finely
 grated
4 oz (110 g) raisins
4 oz (110 g) stoned dates,
 chopped
1 egg, beaten
4 oz (110 g) wholemeal flour
4 oz (110 g) strong white flour
2 teaspoons baking powder
2 teaspoons bicarbonate of soda
1 teaspoon cinnamon, ground
½ teaspoon nutmeg, grated
2 oz (50 g) walnuts, chopped

for the cream-cheese icing
3 oz (75 g) softened butter
3 oz (75 g) full fat cream cheese
6 oz (175 g) icing sugar
½ teaspoon vanilla essence

THE AVAILABILITY OF CARROT CAKE HAS INCREASED GREATLY IN RE-
CENT YEARS PARTICULARLY IN AMERICAN-STYLE RESTAURANTS,
ALTHOUGH MANY OF THE CAKES I'VE TASTED HAVE NOTHING TO
OFFER IN COMPARISON TO THIS FIRST CLASS EXAMPLE.

Preheat the oven to 350°F-180°C-Gas Mark 4.

Grease the bottom of a deep 8″ (20 cm) cake tin and line with non-stick baking parchment.

Add the lemon juice to the milk in a jug and put to one side.

In a medium sized saucepan melt the butter and honey. When melted remove from the heat and add the grated carrots, raisins, dates, beaten egg and reserved soured milk.

Into a large bowl sift the wholemeal and white flour with the baking powder, bicarbonate of soda, cinnamon, nutmeg and bran from the sieve. Make a well in the centre of the flour mixture and pour in the carrot mixture. Stir together until well blended then add the walnuts and pour into the prepared tin.

Bake in the centre of the oven for 1-1½ hours. Leave in the tin to cool partially before turning out on to a rack.

Serve warm or cold. Delicious with the cream-cheese icing.
To make the icing beat all the ingredients together until smooth and spread over the top of the cooled cake. Chill in the fridge for 30 minutes to set the icing.

~

Cheesecake Choice

SERVES 6

for the pastry
6 oz (175 g) plain flour
3 oz (75 g) butter
1 oz (25 g) sugar
1 egg, beaten
pinch of salt

for the filling
8 oz (225 g) cream cheese
3 oz (75 g) sugar
2 eggs, lightly beaten
2 tablespoons self-raising flour
juice of ½ lemon
1 teaspoon vanilla essence
¾ pint (425 ml) full cream milk
2 oz chopped dried apricots or
    prunes (50 g), optional
icing sugar

THIS IS A 'PROPER' OVEN-BAKED CHEESECAKE WHICH I ALWAYS REGARD AS BEING 'THE REAL THING'. IT'S DELICIOUS WITH FRESH CREAM.

Preheat the oven to 375°F-190°C-Gas Mark 5.

Begin by making the pastry. Sieve the flour into a mixing bowl. Add the butter, cut into cubes, and rub in until the mixture resembles crumbs. Add in the sugar, beaten egg and salt and mix everything well together until you have a firm ball of dough.

Grease and flour a spring form tin or flan ring at least 2½" (5 cm) deep. Press the pastry evenly into the base of the flan tin, using your fingers. (This pastry cannot be rolled out.)

Next cream together the cheese and the sugar and blend in the lightly beaten eggs until the mixture is smooth. Beat in the flour and then add the lemon juice and vanilla essence. Gradually whisk in the milk.

If using the dried fruit, scatter this over the pastry base. Pour in the filling. Bake in the oven on a baking tray for 55-60 minutes.

Allow to cool completely and then sprinkle with icing sugar and serve.

~

Cinnamon Surprise Cake

4 oz (110 g) margarine
6 oz (175 g) caster sugar
3 eggs, beaten
10 oz (275 g) plain flour
1 level teaspoon bicarbonate of
    soda
1 level teaspoon baking powder
pinch of salt
5 fl oz (150 ml) natural yoghurt
1 oz (25 g) chopped hazelnuts
1½ oz (40 g) chocolate chips
1 level teaspoon cinnamon
1 oz (25 g) butter
2 oz (50 g) soft brown sugar

HERE'S A CAKE TO TALK ABOUT AND THE SURPRISE IS THAT, INSTEAD OF ACTUALLY BEING IN THE CAKE, THE CINNAMON HELPS TO MAKE UP THE UNUSUAL SWEET AND SLIGHTLY AROMATIC TOPPING. LOVELY.

Preheat the oven to 350°F-180°C-Gas Mark 4.

In a bowl cream together the margarine and sugar. When light and fluffy add the beaten eggs.

In another bowl mix together 8 oz (225 g) of the flour, bicarbonate of soda, baking powder and salt, and then fold gently into the first mixture. Fold in the yoghurt, stir in the chocolate chips with the chopped hazelnuts and pour the mixture into a greased and lined 8" (20 cm) cake tin.

Mix together the remaining 2 oz (50 g) flour with the cinnamon in a bowl. Rub in the butter with fingertips. Stir in the brown sugar. Sprinkle this all over the surface of the cake in the tin and then bake in the preheated oven for 1 hour 10 minutes.

Classic Cheesecake

SERVES about 10

for the base
4 oz (110 g) cake crumbs

for the filling
grated rind of 1 orange
grated rind of 2 lemons
1½ lb (700 g) cream cheese
1 teaspoon vanilla essence
6 oz (175 g) double cream
7 oz (200 g) sugar
4 eggs
2 tablespoons soured cream
2 fl oz (55 ml) single cream

THERE'S QUITE A VAST NUMBER OF CHEESECAKE RECIPES, MANY OF THEM SIMPLY REQUIRING THE 'ASSEMBLE AND CHILL' TREATMENT, AND TRUE, I SUPPOSE, SOME OF THESE ARE FINE, BUT THIS ONE, FOR ME, REALLY LIVES UP TO ITS TITLE.

Grease an 8″ (20 cm) shallow tin and sprinkle the cake crumbs in the base.

In a bowl mix the orange and lemon rinds, cream cheese and vanilla. Beat them together until very smooth. Gradually blend in the double cream and sugar. Add the eggs, one at a time, beating the mixture well after each addition. Mix in the soured and single cream.

Pour into the prepared tin and place in a roasting dish which contains enough boiling water to come halfway up the cake tin. Bake in the oven at 375°F-190°C-Gas Mark 5 for 1 hour, until the centre of the cake is set.

Cool in the tin for 10 minutes then unmould while still hot.

Cool thoroughly before serving.

~

Dundee Cake

4 oz (110 g) currants
4 oz (110 g) sultanas
4 oz (110 g) raisins
4 oz (110 g) chopped mixed peel
10 oz (275 g) plain flour
8 oz (225 g) butter
8 oz (225 g) soft brown sugar
grated rind of 1 lemon
4 eggs, beaten
3 oz (75 g) split almonds

A FAMOUS CAKE, OF COURSE, AND THIS VERSION IS MY PERSONAL FAVOURITE.

Preheat the oven to 325°F-170°C-Gas Mark 3.

In a bowl mix together the dried fruits and the chopped mixed peel. Stir in the flour.

In another bowl cream the butter, sugar and lemon rind until pale and fluffy. Beat in the eggs and then fold in the flour, fruit and peel.

Reserve 1 oz (25 g) of the nuts and chop the rest into pieces. Add the broken nuts to the mixture, stir through well and place the mixture into a greased and lined 8″ (20 cm) cake tin. Arrange the reserved almonds over the top.

Bake in the preheated oven for 2½-3 hours.

~

Honey and Ginger Cheesecake

SERVES 8

for the base
4 oz (110 g) plain flour
pinch of salt
2 oz (50 g) butter
½ oz (10 g) caster sugar
2 tablespoons water

for the filling
8 oz (225 g) cottage cheese,
  sieved
2 tablespoons double cream
1 tablespoon honey
2 egg yolks
2 teaspoons lemon juice
2 egg whites
1 tablespoon chopped candied
  ginger
1 tablespoon chopped glacé
  cherries
3 tablespoons sultanas
pinch of cinnamon
3 oz (75 g) walnuts, finely
  chopped

A GOOD HANDFUL OF SULTANAS IS PROBABLY THE MOST POPULAR ADDITION TO THE STANDARD CHEESECAKE MIX. THIS RECIPE EASILY GOES QUITE A BIT FURTHER WITH WONDERFUL RESULTS.

To make the pastry base sift the flour and salt into a bowl and rub in the butter with the fingertips until the mixture resembles breadcrumbs. Stir in the sugar and then add a little water, using a knife to mix to a pliable dough.

Grease an 8″ (20 cm) loose-bottomed tin, and line with the rolled-out pastry.

In a bowl mix together the cottage cheese, cream, honey, egg yolks and lemon juice.

Whisk the egg whites until they are stiff and fold them through the mixture. Then fold in the ginger, cherries and sultanas. Pour the mixture onto the pastry and sprinkle the top with cinnamon.

Bake in the oven at 425°F-220°C-Gas Mark 7 for just 10 minutes then reduce the heat to 375°F-190°C-Gas Mark 5 and cook for a further 30 minutes. As the cake is cooling sprinkle the nuts over the top.

~

Honey and Nut Delight

6 oz (175 g) shelled almonds
4 oz (110 g) shelled walnuts
8 oz (225 g) chopped mixed peel
¼ teaspoon ground allspice
½ teaspoon ground cinnamon
1 teaspoon ground coriander
5 oz (150 g) plain flour
4 oz (110 g) icing sugar
1 tablespoon water
5 oz (150 g) runny honey

FRANKLY, WHAT WE HAVE HERE COULD COME UNDER THE HEADING OF 'SELF INDULGENCE', ESPECIALLY IF, AFTER CUTTING, YOU COAT THE PIECES ON ONE SIDE WITH DARK MELTED CHOCOLATE AND ALLOW THEM TO SET ON A WIRE RACK. BUT THEN WE ALL DESERVE THE OCCASIONAL TREAT, DON'T WE?

Preheat the oven to 425°F-220°C-Gas Mark 7.

Spread all the nuts on a baking tray and toast in the preheated oven until golden, about 7-10 minutes. Remove from the oven and chop roughly.

Reduce the oven temperature to 375°F-190°C-Gas Mark 5.

Line the base and sides of an 8" (20 cm) loose-bottomed flan dish with rice paper.

Place the chopped mixed peel, the allspice, cinnamon and coriander with the flour in a mixing bowl. Add the toasted nuts and mix well together.

Reserve 1 tablespoon of the icing sugar and put the rest in a saucepan with the water and honey. Stir continuously with a wooden spoon over a low heat until bubbles start to appear on the surface. Remove the mixture from the heat immediately. Gradually stir the fruit and nut mixture into the syrup. Turn into the prepared tin and smooth the surface with a wet knife blade. Sprinkle the top with the reserved icing sugar.

Bake in the oven for 30 minutes.

Allow to cool in the tin before cutting.

~

Madeira Cake

5 oz (150 g) butter
5 oz (150 g) caster sugar
3 eggs, beaten
8 oz (225 g) self-raising flour
juice of ¼ lemon
zest of half a lemon

WHEN I VISITED MADEIRA I DISCOVERED, TO MY SURPRISE, THAT THE LOCAL TRADITIONAL CAKE IS OF THE DARK AND STICKY VARIETY AND QUITE UNLIKE THIS ONE HERE – WHICH HAS THE ADDED INTEREST OF A LEMON ZEST SPRINKLING.

In a bowl cream the butter and sugar together until fluffy. Beat in the eggs with a little of the flour. Add the lemon juice and then fold in the remaining flour.

Place the mixture in a greased 8″ (20 cm) cake tin and bake in the oven at 350°F-180°C-Gas Mark 4 for 1 hour.

After 30 minutes' cooking time carefully scatter the lemon zest over the top of the cake and complete cooking.

~

Malted Fruit Loaf

1 oz (25 g) raisins
2 oz (50 g) sultanas
8 oz (225 g) self-raising flour
4 tablespoons treacle
4 tablespoons malt extract
6 tablespoons milk
1 teaspoon bicarbonate of soda
½ teaspoon nutmeg
1 egg, beaten

I REMEMBER AS A BOY BEING GIVEN MY DAILY ALLOWANCE OF HEALTH-PROMOTING MALT EXTRACT (AVAILABLE FROM THE CHEMIST'S SHOP). THIS FRUITY LOAF, WITH ADDED TREACLE, TASTES EVEN BETTER WITH A GENEROUS SPREADING OF BUTTER.

Put the raisins and sultanas in a large mixing bowl, and stir together. Add the flour and mix well.

In a saucepan warm together the treacle and malt extract, then stir in the milk, bicarbonate of soda, nutmeg and beaten egg.

Pour this mixture on to the fruit and stir everything together well. Pour the mixture into a greased and lined 2 lb (1 kg) loaf tin.

Bake in the oven at 350°F-180°C-Gas Mark 4 for 45 minutes.

~

Mystery Cake

6 oz (175 g) butter or
    margarine, softened
6 oz (175 g) light brown sugar
12 oz (350 g) plain flour
3 teaspoons baking powder
2 teaspoons mixed spice
½ teaspoon freshly grated
    nutmeg
1 teaspoon bicarbonate of soda
½ teaspoon salt
4 oz (110 g) sultanas or raisins
10½ oz (295 g) can condensed
    tomato soup
6 fl oz (175 ml) water
4 oz (110 g) walnuts, coarsely
    chopped

JUST FOR FUN, DON'T TELL ANYONE ABOUT THE TOMATO SOUP UNTIL THEY'VE PRONOUNCED IT DELICIOUS – THAT'S JUST THE MOMENT TO REVEAL THE 'MYSTERY' INGREDIENT. IT'S A VERY NICE CAKE.

Preheat the oven to 350°F-180°C-Gas Mark 4.

In a bowl cream the butter and sugar together until they become as fluffy as possible.

In another bowl sift the flour with the baking powder, mixed spice, nutmeg, bicarbonate of soda and salt. Toss the sultanas in this mixture and remove them with a slotted spoon and keep separately.

Stir the dry ingredients into the butter and sugar mixture and beat well. Then beat in the tomato soup and the water and mix again. Carefully stir the floured sultanas and the nuts into the batter.

Grease and flour an 8″ (20 cm) or 9″ (23 cm) cake tin and pour in the batter. Bake in the oven for about 1 hour until a thin skewer thrust into the centre comes out clean.

Cool the cake in the tin for 10 minutes before turning out on to a rack.

~

Pineapple Cake

4 oz (110 g) butter
6 oz (110 g) soft brown sugar
7 oz (200 g) can crushed
    pineapple, drained
12 oz (350 g) mixed dried fruit
4 oz (110 g) glacé cherries
8 oz (225 g) self-raising flour
1 teaspoon mixed spice
2 eggs, beaten

IF YOU HAVE NEVER BAKED A CAKE BEFORE THEN THIS IS THE ONE TO START WITH. I HAVE NEVER KNOWN IT TO FAIL, OR NOT TO PLEASE.

Put the butter, sugar, pineapple, mixed dried fruit and glacé cherries into a saucepan. Heat gently together and allow to melt. Increase the heat until the mixture comes to the boil. Take off the heat and leave to cool.

When cool, stir in the sifted flour and mixed spice. Mix in the beaten eggs and blend everything well together.

Pour into a greased 7″ (18 cm) cake tin and bake in the oven at 300°F-150°C-Gas Mark 2 for 1 hour 35 minutes.

NOTE:In the unlikely event of finding crushed pineapple unavailable, simply whizz up in a blender a similar sized can of pineapple chunks or rings with their juice, then drain and proceed.

Quick Christmas Cake

8 oz (225 g) margarine
6 oz (175 g) soft brown sugar
2 rounded tablespoons set honey
5 eggs
4 oz (110 g) chopped mixed peel
2 oz (50 g) blanched almonds
4 oz (110 g) glacé cherries,
    chopped
8 oz (225 g) currants
8 oz (225 g) raisins
8 oz (225 g) sultanas
9 oz (250 g) plain flour
1 level teaspoon baking powder
1 level teaspoon nutmeg
½ level teaspoon cinnamon
½ level teaspoon cloves,
    powdered
3 tablespoons – ¼ cup brandy
    or rum or sherry (optional)

for the icing
8 oz (225 g) sieved icing sugar
1 tablespoon lemon juice
1 tablespoon warm water
glacé cherries
angelica

THIS IS THE CHRISTMAS CAKE THE ANTHONY FAMILY HAS RELIED ON FOR SEVERAL YEARS NOW, AND WE ALL LOVE IT. IT CAN BE MADE AS LATE AS TWO OR THREE DAYS BEFORE EATING AND BECAUSE IT'S MADE IN A RING TIN IT'S VERY EASY TO SLICE. THE SIMPLE DECORATION LOOKS VERY EFFECTIVE, ESPECIALLY WITH A SPRIG OF HOLLY IN THE CENTRE OPENING. DURING BAKING, THE MIXTURE RISES ABOVE THE RIM OF THE RING BUT AS IT'S PRESENTED UPSIDE DOWN THIS DOESN'T MATTER AT ALL.

Simply put all the ingredients, except the brandy, together in a large mixing bowl and stir thoroughly for 3 minutes until everything is well combined together.

Grease and flour a 9" (23 cm) ring tin. Put the cake mixture into the tin, and smooth over the top. Bake in a slow oven, 300°F-150°C-Gas Mark 2 for 2½ hours. Leave to cool in the tin for 15 minutes before turning out on to a wire tray.

Prick the surface of the cake with a skewer and if wished sprinkle over either brandy, rum or sherry. The amount can be anything from 3 to 5 tablespoons.

Cover the cake completely in foil or cling film and store in an airtight tin.

To finish the cake, put the icing sugar in a bowl and stir in the lemon juice and enough warm water to make a stiff pouring consistency. Pour it over the top of the cake and allow the icing to run, unevenly down the sides of the cake.

Decorate the top of the cake with glacé cherries and leaves cut from the angelica.

~

Simnel Cake

6 oz (175 g) butter
6 oz (175 g) brown sugar
3 eggs, beaten
9 oz (250 g) self-raising flour
pinch of salt
½ teaspoon mixed spice
5 tablespoons milk
2 teaspoons golden syrup
1 lb (450 g) currants
2 oz (50 g) raisins
4 oz (110 g) sultanas
1 oz (25 g) glacé cherries,
   quartered
4 oz (110 g) mixed peel, chopped
1 lb (450 g) almond paste
apricot jam

TRADITIONALLY THIS IS A EASTER-TIME TREAT, HISTORICALLY CENTRED ON MOTHERING SUNDAY. THE ALMOND PASTE BALLS FOR THE TOPPING ARE SAID TO REPRESENT THE APOSTLES MINUS POOR OLD JUDAS WHO TOOK THE MONEY AND RAN. HE SHOULD HAVE STAYED, IT'S A VERY GOOD CAKE.

Beat the butter and sugar together until light and fluffy. Add the beaten eggs, one at a time with a little flour, beating well after each addition. Stir in the salt and spice. Add the milk and syrup with a little more flour. Fold in the remaining flour and the fruit and peel.

Place half the mixture into a greased and lined 8" (20 cm) round cake tin and smooth level.

Divide the almond paste into two. Roll out one piece to 8" (20 cm) in diameter on sugared greaseproof and place this on top of the cake mixture. Cover with the remaining cake mixture.

Bake in the oven at 350°F-180°C-Gas Mark 4 for 1 hour and then reduce the oven temperature to 275°F-140°C-Gas Mark 1 for a further 2½ hours.

Allow the cake to cool then divide the remaining almond paste into two. Roll one half to an 8" (20 cm) round. Brush the cake with apricot jam and place the paste on top.

Roll the remaining paste into eleven small balls. Brush the top of the cake with beaten egg and place the balls of paste round the edge, close together, then brush again with egg.

Place on a baking tray and return to the oven for 10-15 minutes to brown the top very lightly.

~

The 'Special' Cake

2 oz (50 g) sultanas
2 oz (50 g) raisins
2 oz (50 g) currants
2 oz (50 g) stoned dates,
    chopped
2 oz (50g) polyunsaturated
    margarine
plus extra for greasing
¼ pint (150 ml) skimmed milk
1 egg, beaten
5 oz (150 ml) wholemeal flour
2 teaspoons baking powder
1 teaspoon ground cinnamon
1 teaspoon ground nutmeg
approx 4 tablespoons skimmed
    milk

THIS CAKE IS 'SPECIAL' BECAUSE IT TAKES INTO CONSIDERATION THE FACT THAT SOME OF US, FOR HEALTH REASONS, HAVE TO AVOID SUGAR, BUT STILL WANT TO HAVE OUR CAKE AND EAT IT.

Preheat the oven to 350°F-180°C-Gas Mark 4.

Grease and line a 7" (18 cm) cake tin.

Put the dried fruit, margarine and ¼ pint (150 ml) milk in a saucepan and bring slowly to the boil. Reduce the heat and simmer gently, covered, for 10 minutes. Remove from the heat and allow to cool.

Stir in the egg. Gradually mix in the flour with the baking powder, cinnamon and nutmeg and enough skimmed milk to give a dropping consistency.

Pour the mixture into the prepared cake tin and bake in the oven for 30 minutes until risen and firm to the touch.

Cool on a wire tray.

~

Yoghurt Cake

1 × 5 fl oz (150 ml) carton
    natural yoghurt
1 × 5 fl oz (150 ml) carton
    cooking oil
2 × 5 fl oz (300 g) carton caster
    sugar
3 × 5 fl oz (450 g) carton self-
    raising flour
3 eggs
2-3 drops vanilla essence
grated zest and juice of 1 lemon
    or orange or
2-3 oz (50-75 oz) sultanas

ONE OF MY WIFE'S GREAT FAVOURITES. THE REALLY HANDY FEATURE HERE IS THAT THE EMPTIED YOGHURT POT IS USED TO MEASURE OUT THE OIL, SUGAR AND FLOUR. (SIMPLY RINSE AND WIPE DRY AFTER ADDING THE OIL.) TRULY A MINOR MASTERPIECE.

Preheat the oven to 325°F-170°C-Gas Mark 3.

In a bowl mix together the yoghurt, cooking oil, caster sugar and self-raising flour. Add the three whole eggs and mix in well. Then add either 2-3 drops of vanilla essence and the grated rind and juice of a lemon or orange – or add the sultanas, if preferred.

Pour the mixture into a greaseproof lined 2 lb (900 g) loaf tin and bake in the oven for 2 hours.

Delicious spread with butter.

~

PUDDINGS

Apple and Almond Tarts

MAKES 6

for the pastry
8 oz (225 g) plain flour
pinch of salt
4 oz (110 g) butter
1 egg
cold water to mix

for the filling
1 lb (450 g) cooking apples
2 oz (50 g) margarine
2 oz (50 g) golden syrup
2 oz (50 g) almonds, roughly
  chopped

SERVED STILL WARM FROM THE OVEN THESE ARE TRULY SCRUMP-
TIOUS – AND WITH A DOLLOP OF THICK CREAM, ECSTASY.

First make the pastry. Sift the flour into a bowl with the salt, then
add the butter cut into small pieces. Rub the butter into the flour
until the mixture resembles fine breadcrumbs.

Beat the egg and add gradually, with a very little water, to the
crumb mixture until you have a firm dough. Leave to rest in a cool
place while you make the filling.

Peel, core and slice the apples. Place them in a saucepan with
the margarine and golden syrup and cook together gently until
the apples are tender. Allow to cool and then stir in the roughly
chopped almonds. Roll out the pastry on a lightly floured board
and use to line six 3″ (7.5 cm) individual tart tins. Fill each one with
a sixth of the apple and almond mixture.

Bake in the oven at 400°F-200°C-Gas Mark 6 for 10-15 minutes,
then serve warm.

~

Blackberry and Apple Pie

SERVES 4

for the pastry
6 oz (175 g) plain flour
4 oz (110 g) butter
1 tablespoon caster sugar
1 egg yolk
cold water to mix

for the filling
2 lb (900 g) cooking apples
2 tablespoons cornflour
6 oz (175 g) blackberries
4 oz (110 g) granulated sugar
1 teaspoon ground cinnamon

for the top
lightly beaten egg white
sugar to sprinkle

JUST THE THING FOR KEENER AUTUMN APPETITES WHEN THE FRUITS ARE AT THEIR SEASONAL BEST. THE ADDITION OF CORNFLOUR HELPS THICKEN THE JUICES DURING BAKING.

To make the sweet pastry sift the flour into a bowl. Add the butter cut into small pieces and rub in with the fingertips until the mixture resembles breadcrumbs. Stir in the sugar. Mix the egg yolk with 1 tablespoon cold water and stir into the mixture using a round-bladed knife to form a firm dough. Chill for 20 minutes before using.

Peel and core the apples and then slice them thinly and coat them in the cornflour. Place them in the 2 pint (1.25 litre) pie dish in layers with the blackberries, sugar and cinnamon, finishing with a layer of apples.

Roll out the pastry slightly larger than the rim of the pie dish. Cut a strip from the edge of the pastry and lay it on the dampened rim of the dish. Dampen the edges of the remaining pastry and place on the top of the pie, pressing the two pastry edges together. Trim the pastry and knock up the edges. Make a small slit in the centre of the pastry lid and decorate, if wished, with any trimmings. Brush the pastry top with the beaten egg white and sprinkle with some sugar.

Bake the pie in the oven at 400°F-200°C-Gas Mark 6 for the first 20 minutes then reduce the oven temperature to 350°F-180°C-Gas Mark 4 for a further 30 minutes or until the apples are tender.

~

Butterscotch Ice-cream

SERVES 8

6 tablespoons soft dark brown
  sugar
2 oz (50 g) butter
½ pint (275 ml) warm milk
2 eggs
2½ oz (60 g) granulated sugar
1 teaspoon vanilla essence
½ pint (275 ml) whipping
  cream
flaked almonds, toasted

A TREAT TO MAKE ANY OCCASION EXTRA SPECIAL.

Warm the brown sugar and butter in a saucepan until both have melted. Allow to bubble for 1 minute. Add the warm milk and heat gently, stirring, until everything is well blended.

In a bowl beat the eggs and the granulated sugar until well mixed, and stir in the warm milk and vanilla essence. Strain back into the saucepan. Stir over a low heat until the custard thickens slightly. Do not boil. Cool.

Lightly whip the cream and mix into the custard. Pour into a container and freeze until mushy. Beat well and then return to the freezer until firm.

When serving, decorate with a topping of browned, flaked almonds.

~

Chocolate Mud Pudding

SERVES 6

4 oz (110 g) self-raising flour
2 oz (50 g) caster sugar
½ teaspoon salt
2 oz (50 g) butter
1 oz (25 g) chocolate (dark is
  best but milk can be used)
1 teaspoon vanilla essence
¼ pint (150 ml) milk
4 tablespoons cocoa powder
4 oz (110 g) dark brown sugar
½ pint (275 ml) cold water

I COULD SAY THIS WOULD SERVE FROM TWO TO SIX PEOPLE, A RATHER ELASTIC SERVINGS FIGURE, BECAUSE WHEN I DEMONSTRATED THIS ON TV-AM, ASTROLOGER RUSSELL GRANT, A SELF-CONFESSED 'CHOCA-HOLIC', ENJOYED IT SO *VERY* MUCH.

Preheat the oven to 350°F-180°C-Gas Mark 4.

In a bowl mix together the sifted flour, sugar and salt.

Put the butter and chocolate together in a saucepan and heat gently until both are melted. Stir in the vanilla essence and the milk. Allow to cool and then stir into the flour mixture. Pour the batter into a 2 pint (1.25 litre) pudding bowl or deep dish.

In a bowl mix the cocoa powder and brown sugar together and then spoon this over the top of the batter. Pat gently with the back of the spoon until level. Pour the ½ pint (275 ml) cold water straight over the top of the pudding.

Bake in the oven for about 45 minutes until the sponge has risen and the liquid lies underneath as a thick chocolate sauce.

Very good with ice-cream or cream.

~

Frangipan Tart

SERVES 6

for the pastry
6 oz (175 g) self-raising flour
pinch of salt
3 oz (75 g) butter
cold water to mix

3 tablespoons apricot jam

for the filling
2 eggs, beaten
4 oz (110 g) butter, softened
4 oz (110 g) caster sugar
4 oz (110 g) almonds
2 teaspoons almond essence
icing sugar

I THINK OF THIS AS A FRIENDLY FIRST COUSIN TO DERBYSHIRE'S FAMOUS BAKEWELL TART AND A VERY PLEASANT RELATIONSHIP IT IS TOO.

For the pastry base sift the flour and salt into a bowl. Add the butter cut into small dice and rub in until the mixture resembles breadcrumbs. Add 1 or 2 tablespoons cold water to mix to a firm dough. Roll out on a lightly floured board and use to line a greased 8" (20 cm) flan tin.

Spread the apricot jam over the base of the pastry.

Place the ingredients for the filling (with the exception of the icing sugar) in a bowl and beat everything well together. Spoon the mixture into the flan case and bake in the oven at 350°F-180°C-Gas Mark 4 for 40 minutes until the filling is set.

Dust the top with sifted icing sugar and leave to cool in the tin.

~

French Apple Tart

SERVES 6

for the pastry
8 oz (225 g) plain flour
pinch of salt
4 oz (110 g) butter
1 egg
cold water to mix

for the filling
2 lb (900 g) cooking apples
4-5 oz (110-150 g) sugar
2 tablespoons apricot jam

BASICALLY SIMPLE BUT LOOKS SO GOOD THAT PEOPLE WILL ASK WHERE IT WAS BOUGHT. THE SECRET LIES IN THINLY SLICING THE APPLE QUARTERS.

Sift the flour into a bowl with a pinch of salt. Dice the butter into the flour and mix to a fine crumble. Beat the egg and add it to the mixture gradually, together with a little water, until you have a firm pastry ball. Knead a little and then leave to rest in a cool place for about 2 hours.

Meanwhile peel, core and quarter the apples, then slice them very finely.

Roll out the pastry.

Lightly butter a 9-10" (23-25.5 cm) tart tin and line it with the pastry. Make a few incisions with the point of a sharp knife or a fork. Arrange the apples in circles, overlapping, starting from the outside edge, and sprinkle each layer with sugar.

Bake in a moderate oven, 375°F-190°C-Gas Mark 5, for 30 minutes. Test the apples with the tip of a sharp knife – and if still hard cook for a further 10 minutes.

Melt the apricot jam in a pan and brush over the surface of the tart, to glaze.

Ginger Pudding

SERVES 6

8 oz (225 g) self-raising flour
pinch of salt
2 teaspoons ground ginger
2 oz (50 g) margarine
2 oz (50 g) sugar
2 tablespoons treacle
2 eggs
1 oz (25 g) stem ginger,
  chopped

STEAMING SEEMS TO BE MAKING A WELCOME RETURN, ESPECIALLY FOR COOKING VEGETABLES. STEAMED PUDDINGS, ALTHOUGH THEY DO TAKE TIME AND SOME ATTENTION, CERTAINLY REPAY THE EFFORT BOTH IN TASTE AND APPRECIATION.

In a bowl mix together the flour, salt and ginger. Cut the margarine into dice and rub it into the flour mixture. Add the sugar, treacle, 2 eggs and the stem ginger to the bowl, and mix everything well together.

Place the mixture in a greased 1½ pint (750 ml) pudding basin. Cover it with greaseproof paper or foil and steam the pudding for 2 hours.

~

Jam Pudding

SERVES 6

4 oz (110 g) margarine
4 oz (110 g) caster sugar
2 eggs
8 oz (225 g) self-raising flour
2 tablespoons milk
3 tablespoons jam

ANOTHER LOVELY EXAMPLE OF THE TRADITIONAL AND COMFORTING PUDDING THAT'S ALWAYS WONDERFUL TO COME HOME TO.

Cream the margarine and sugar together until pale and fluffy. Beat in the eggs. Fold in the flour with the milk, and mix carefully until everything is well blended together.

Grease a 1½ pint (750 ml) pudding basin and place the jam in the base of the basin. Pour in the pudding mixture and cover with greaseproof paper or foil and steam for 2 hours.

~

Lemon Meringue Pie

for the pastry
4 oz (110 g) plain flour
pinch of salt
2 oz (50 g) butter
½ oz (10 g) caster sugar
cold water to mix

for the filling
2 eggs, separated
8 oz (225 g) caster sugar
juice and grated rind of 1 lemon
¼ pint (150 ml) boiling water
1 oz (25 g) cornflour

A DELICIOUS COMBINATION OF LIGHT AND CRISP MERINGUE TOPPING WHICH GENTLY GIVES WAY TO THE SMOOTH LEMONY FILLING AND SWEET SHORTCRUST PASTRY. IN THE METHOD THE INSTRUCTION TO 'CUT IN' THE BUTTER MEANS THAT YOU ADD THE BUTTER TO THE BOWL OF FLOUR IN ONE PIECE AND THEN USE A KNIFE TO CUT IT INTO SMALL PIECES IN THE FLOUR, THEREBY KEEPING THE BUTTER AS FIRM AND COLD AS POSSIBLE.

Sieve the flour and salt into a bowl. Cut in the butter and rub in with the fingertips to resemble breadcrumbs. Stir in the sugar and enough water to form a stiff dough. Leave for 20 minutes before using.

Roll out the pastry on a lightly floured board and use to line a greased 7" (18 cm) fluted flan tin. Line with greaseproof paper and baking beans and bake 'blind' for 10 minutes at 350°F-180°C-Gas Mark 4. Remove the paper and beans and return to the oven for a further 5 minutes.

In a saucepan beat the egg yolks with 4 oz (110 g) of the sugar until creamy. Add the lemon juice, grated rind and the boiling water. Mix the cornflour to a smooth paste with a little cold water and blend into the egg mixture. Bring everything almost to the boil, stirring well. Pour into the baked flan case.

Whisk the egg whites until stiff, and gradually beat in the remaining sugar. Spread over the top of the flan and bake in the oven at 300°F-150°C-Gas Mark 2 for 25-30 minutes until crisp and pale golden brown.

~

Mince Pies

Makes 20

8 oz rough puff pastry
mincemeat

BEFORE, DURING AND EVEN AFTER THE CHRISTMAS SEASON THESE ARE ALWAYS ESPECIALLY WELCOME. FOR EXTRA ENJOYMENT POP A TEASPOONFUL OF WHIPPED CREAM, FLAVOURED WITH A LITTLE BRANDY OR RUM, ON TOP.

Roll out the pastry on a lightly floured surface until it is very thin. Using two cutters, one slightly larger than the other, cut out 20 small rounds and then 20 of the larger rounds, re-rolling the trimmings for use.

Place the 20 smaller rounds on lightly greased baking sheets and then put a small spoonful of the mincemeat on each one. Dampen the edges and then cover each one with the larger rounds, sealing the edges together well.

Brush the tops with beaten egg or milk and make a small hole in the top of each pie. Bake in the oven at 450°F-230°C-Gas Mark 8 for about 15 minutes.

~

Norwegian Apple Cake

Serves 4

2 large eggs
9 oz (250 g) caster sugar
4 oz (110 g) butter
¼ pint (150 ml) full cream milk
6 oz (175 g) plain flour
3 teaspoons baking powder
4 cooking apples

MORE A PUDDING THAN A CAKE REALLY, BUT WITH SOMETHING AS GOOD AS THIS 'WHAT'S IN A NAME?'.

Preheat the oven to 400°F-200°C-Gas Mark 6.

Whisk the eggs with 8 oz (225 g) of the caster sugar until they are thick and creamy and leave a trail when the whisk is lifted.

Cut the butter into dice and place in a saucepan with the milk and heat gently before bringing to the boil. Remove from the heat and stir in the egg and sugar mixture. Sieve the flour and baking powder together and fold them gently into the batter. Pour the mixture into a well-buttered 8″ × 12″ (20 × 30 cm) tin.

Peel, core and slice the apples and place the slices in rows along the top of the pudding.

Bake in the oven for 20-25 minutes until well risen and golden brown.

Delicious hot or cold with cream.

~

Roly Poly Pudding

SERVES 4

8 oz (225 g) suet pastry
4 tablespoons jam, syrup or
marmalade

FOR COMPLETE SATISFACTION ALL THIS NEEDS IS PLENTY OF PIPING
HOT CUSTARD.

Roll out the pastry on a floured surface into a rectangle 10" × 8"
(25.5 × 20 cm). Spread with jam, syrup or marmalade, up to 1" (2.5
cm) from the edges. (This will prevent the jam from burning.)

Moisten the edges of the pastry with water and roll up loosely
from the narrow end. Press the edges together to seal.

Lift the roll on to a greased baking sheet and bake at
400°F-200°C-Gas Mark 6 for 30-35 minutes.

~

Soured Cream, Walnut and Date Pie

SERVES 6

for the pastry
7 oz (200 g) plain flour
salt
3½ oz (100 g) butter
3 tablespoons cold water to mix

for the filling
½ pint (275 ml) soured cream
1 egg, beaten
2 oz (50 g) light brown sugar
8 oz (225 g) pitted dates, finely
chopped
3 oz (75 g) walnuts, chopped
1 teaspoon grated lemon rind

THIS COULD BE THE PERFECT ANSWER TO A SEARCH FOR SOMETHING
'A LITTLE BIT DIFFERENT'.

Sift the flour and a pinch of salt into a bowl. Dice the butter into
the flour and rub it in until the mixture resembles breadcrumbs.
Mix to a dough with the water. Roll out on a floured surface and
then line a buttered 8" (20 cm) tart tin with the pastry. Cut the left-
over dough into long strips for the top of the tart.

For the filling put the soured cream into a mixing bowl. Add the
beaten egg and the brown sugar and mix well together. Then add
the pitted dates, chopped walnuts and grated lemon rind and stir
through. Pour the mixture into the unbaked pie shell.

Arrange the dough strips across the pie forming a lattice de-
sign. Brush these strips with egg white.

Bake in a hot oven 425°F-220°C-Gas Mark 7 for just 10 minutes,
then reduce the oven temperature to 325°F-170°C-Gas Mark 3 and
continue cooking until the filling is set and the crust lightly
browned (about 30 minutes).

Serve with unsweetened whipped cream.

~

Spotted Dick

SERVES 4

4 oz (110 g) self-raising flour
pinch of salt
2 oz (50 g) shredded suet
2 oz (50 g) caster sugar
2 oz (50 g) currants
2 oz (50 g) mixed peel
1 egg, beaten
4 tablespoons milk

EVERYONE HAS HEARD OF THIS BUT WHEN DID YOU LAST TREAT YOURSELF TO SOME? NOW'S YOUR CHANCE.

In a large bowl mix together all the dry ingredients. Beat in the egg and sufficient milk to give a soft dropping consistency.

Grease a 1 pint (0.55 litre) pudding basin and pour in the pudding mixture. Cover with pleated greaseproof paper and foil and steam for 1½-2 hours.

~

Vanilla Ice-cream

SERVES 8

1 pint (570 ml) milk
1 vanilla pod or few drops of
  essence
6 egg yolks
6 oz (175 g) granulated sugar
1 pint (570 ml) whipping cream

THE DEMAND FOR REAL DAIRY ICE-CREAM IS ON THE INCREASE, PROVING THAT QUALITY NEVER GOES FAR OUT OF FASHION. THIS CLASSIC VANILLA FLAVOUR RECIPE IS ONE OF THE VERY BEST.

Bring the milk and the vanilla pod (or essence) almost to the boil. Take off the heat and leave for at least 15 minutes.

In a bowl beat the egg yolks and sugar together, stir in the milk and then strain back into the pan. Cook this custard gently over a low heat, stirring until it coats the back of a wooden spoon. Do not boil. Pour into a chilled, shallow container and leave to cool. Freeze until slushy – about 2 hours. Remove from the freezer and turn into a large basin and mash with a fork.

In another bowl lightly whip the cream. Fold the cream into the first mixture and freeze again until slushy, remove from the freezer and mash again. Return to the freezer and leave to become firm.

~

Here are two pastry recipes for everyday use – Rough Puff is similar to Flaky Pastry but easier to make. It will keep in the refrigerator for three days or frozen for six months. Suet Pastry, which is usually steamed or boiled, can be used for both traditional sweet and savoury dishes, and for quicker cooking times the fillings should be precooked where necessary.

Rough Puff Pastry

8 oz (225 g) plain flour
½ teaspoon salt
5 oz (150 g) butter or butter
  lard and margarine mixed
cold water to mix

In a bowl mix the flour and salt together. Add the fat, cut into small pieces. Stir in with knife (do not rub in). Gradually add a little water (approx ¼ pint/150 ml), and mix to a stiff dough.

Roll out on to a floured surface into a rectangle. Fold the pastry in three and then turn the open end towards you and roll out again. Repeat this process twice more. Cover the pastry and leave to rest for about 15 minutes. It is then ready for use.

~

Suet Pastry

8 oz (225 g) self-raising flour
pinch of salt
4 oz (110 g) shredded suet
cold water to mix

In a bowl mix together the flour, salt and suet. Add sufficient cold water to make a soft dough. Turn it out on to a floured board and knead lightly.

Allow to rest for a few minutes before rolling out.

This type of pastry is very quick to make and at its best when freshly baked.

~